Questions Catechists Ask
and
Answers That Really Work

---

by Carl J. Pfeifer
and
Janaan Manternach

Sheed & Ward

Sheed & Ward™ is a service of The National Catholic Reporter Publishing Company.

ISBN: 1-55612-620-4

Published by: Sheed & Ward
             115 E. Armour Blvd.
             P.O. Box 419492
             Kansas City, MO 64141

To order, call: (800) 333-7373

Contents

Teaching

is

learning

times

two—

or

more.

We gratefully dedicate this book
to our brothers and sisters,
who are continually for us,
not only as family,
but as friends—
Richard and Rosemary Pfeifer
Orland and LuAnn Manternach
Thomas and Cecilia (deceased) Manternach
Janet Manternach Ripple (deceased)
Donald and Anita Manternach
Grace Manternach Miller

Introduction

QUESTIONS ARE, IN MANY WAYS, MORE IMPORTANT THAN AN-
swers, and any answer that does not flow from and touch down
on a question cannot be very helpful or illuminating.

The theologian Karl Rahner even suggested that questions
are signs of the transcendent God at work in our minds and
hearts.

Our experience leads us to agree heartily with Karl Rahner.
We have come to believe that questions reveal the Holy Spirit's
gentle, creative guidance in people's lives. A large part of
catechesis and other ministries is to evoke questions as much as
to answer them, and to refrain from giving answers to questions
that are not being asked.

Since 1987 we have been writing "Catechists' Questions,"
a regular feature in the monthly newspaper, *The Catechists'
Connection*. In it we respond to some of the questions catechists most frequently ask.

Most of the questions and answers in this book have already appeared there. Others may appear in forthcoming issues.
All have been reedited for inclusion in the present book and re-
arranged in a more logical order, both for personal reading and
for use in catechist formation or in-service programs.

This book is a sequel to our earlier book of questions and
answers, *How To Be a Better Catechist* (1989), which has
helped many catechists as they face new situations and new
questions. We hope the present book will be equally helpful.

The Chapters may be read as interest or need suggests. We
have tried to be as practical as possible.

We want to pass on to other catechists what others have so graciously shared with us by their questions, experience, learning and wisdom. To that we add what we have learned through our own successes and failures.

We want to thank Jean-Marie Hiesberger, editor of *The Catechists' Connection* and her husband, Robert Heyer, editor-in-chief of Sheed & Ward, for encouraging us to write the monthly "Catechists' Questions" feature and the book, *How To Be A Better Catechist*, as well as this present volume.

Carl J. Pfeifer, D.Min.
Janaan Manternach, D.Min.

Arlington, VA
July, 1993

A Catechist's Prayer
for her Learners

I give thanks to my God
for all my memories of you. . . .
And this is my prayer for you:
May your love grow richer and richer yet,
in the fullness of its knowledge
and the depth of its perception,
so that you may learn to prize what is of value:
may nothing cloud your progress:
may you reap through Jesus Christ,
the full harvest.
To God's honor and praise.

—Philippians 1:3, 11

A Learner's Experience
of a Good Catechist

*I shall come again
because I like myself better
when I am with you.*

—Chilean Indian Farewell

Part I

Who? What? Why?

1.

What Do Good Catechists Look Like?

"Our pastor and DRE are calling for volunteers to teach religion to children, adolescents and adults in our parish. I'm tempted, but I keep wondering what kind of a person makes a good catechist."

Think back to the religion teachers and catechists who have most touched you. What were they like? What was it about them that drew you to them? What made them so attractive and effective?

Their qualities may include the following which we have observed in good catechists:

(1) Caring/Loving. Perhaps the most important quality for good catechists is the ability to see each of those they teach as unique, valuable, lovable and worthy of their unconditional love and care. Catechists reveal Christ's love most meaningfully through their own love.

What is important is that those we teach actually feel that we love them and really care.

(2) Reverent/respectful. Good catechists approach each individual with reverence, respecting the dignity and rights, the gifts and fragility of each, with a desire to draw out the best that often lies hidden. A banner we like says, "I like people who handle flowers with care." We hope catechists and all teachers will handle children and young people with care and reverence.

(3) Committed/faithful. Good catechists sincerely work at growing in their commitment to Jesus Christ as they grapple with life's mysteries and challenges. They are prayerful, nurtur-

ing their relationship with Christ through prayer of whatever kinds they find helpful. Their faith in the risen Lord and his message is what catechists are called to share with others.

Good catechists are also faithful to the Church, while acknowledging human failings in the community of Jesus' followers.

They are equally faithful and committed to those they teach.

(4) Understanding/Approachable. Good catechists work at being understanding and approachable, accepting and tolerant, while witnessing honestly to the Church's teachings and their own convictions and values. Their understanding attitude inspires confidence, a growing self-acceptance and healthy questioning.

This quality is even more important in the pluralistic, diverse world in which we live. Those we teach are often different from us in age, culture, experience, race, and point of view. They often bear heavy burdens, hardships and fears, for which simple answers or naive approaches are inadequate.

(5) Open/Questioning. Effective catechists tend to wonder at the mysteries of life and are open to change, to new possibilities and ways of doing things, while respecting the Church's tradition and their own past experience.

Their openness shows itself in a willingness to learn, and to work at expanding the range and depth of their knowledge. They realize neither they nor the Church knows everything or has all the answers. They find time to read, to study, to participate occasionally in conferences and classes.

(6) Creative. Good catechists are not boring. They continually use poetry, story, music, art, and beauty of all kinds as well as activities that stimulate their own and the students' imaginations.

It is not that such catechists are creative geniuses; it is just that they keep working at interesting, attractive, stimulating ways of drawing their students and the Gospel of Jesus Christ into a meaningful interaction. They recognize that people learn through what they see, touch and mold as well as through what they hear.

(7) Enthusiastic. Whether quiet or outgoing, introvert or extrovert, good catechists convey a sense of excitement and enthusiasm about the "good news" of Jesus Christ which they value and wish to share with others. Genuine enthusiasm is more a matter of faith than personality.

(8) Persevering. Good catechists tend to be willing to evaluate and try anew, and are able to cope with difficulties and frustration. They believe in the commitment they have made and don't give up in hard times. Good catechists also refuse to give up on individuals or classes that seem less receptive, negative or hostile.

(9) Happy/Smiling. The news we bring, the Word we are called to echo as catechists, is good news. A catechist's smile says without words that she or he finds in Christ and Christ's way happiness and joy—even, perhaps especially, if that joy and happiness coexist with life's inevitable hurts.

(10) Sense of humor. Few catechists survive long or become successful without a sense of humor. So many unexpected and incongruous things happen in the interaction between catechists and those being catechized that only a sense of humor helps "the medicine go down."

These are ten qualities we look for in catechists, because they describe what good catechists we have known look like.

A somewhat similar list of qualities is found in Chapter 9 of the *National Catechetical Directory.* St. Paul, in Galatians 5:22-23, lists similar qualities as "fruits of the Holy Spirit."

2.

How Be a More Effective Catechist?

"As I look back over last year and look forward to a new year, I keep wondering what I might do to become a more effective catechist. Do you have any helpful hints?"

It just happens that we recently read Stephen R. Covey's best-seller, *The 7 Habits of Highly Effective People.* We will respond to your question by freely adapting Covey's seven habits to catechesis.

Covey stresses that becoming an effective person is more a matter of "character," of personal qualities and habits, than of any quick-fix techniques. Each of the seven habits involves *knowledge* (what to do and why to do it), *skills* (how to do it) and *desire* (wanting to do it).

(1) Be proactive. This means taking initiative and responsibility for your own catechetical ministry, rather than just reacting to situations or being controlled by others.

Being proactive grows out of a sense of confidence in your ability to be an effective catechist. Responsibility (response-ability) and commitment replace "I can't," with "I can," "I choose," "I will."

Be aware of your dignity as a catechist. You are called by Christ and the Church to the vital ministry of echoing God's Word through your actions and words. With your talents, God's help, and the parish's support, you can do just that.

Cherish your call to ministry, and accept your personal responsibility for living out that ministry with confidence and commitment.

(2) Begin with the end in mind. To become a more effective catechist, you need to clarify what you want to accomplish. Learn what your parish community and its leaders expect catechists to be and do.

Then make this personal. Take some quiet time to visualize what it is you want to become and to do as a catechist. What do you hope to see happen in yourself and in those you teach?

Write this down as your mission statement, in your own words, expressing your vision, sense of direction, and values. Look at it from time to time during the year.

(3) Put first things first. To become and do what you have envisioned and committed yourself to requires practical, consistent action.

Putting first things first involves planning. It is a matter of focusing your time and energy on what is important, of scheduling your priorities, rather than simply going along haphazardly.

Plan your catechetical work carefully, focusing on results. Do some long-term planning for the year. Then plan on a weekly basis. Plan your next class right after you finish the previous one.

(4) Think "Win/Win." Catechizing involves other people— those you teach, other catechists, parents, your DRE/CRE or principal, your pastor, and others, too. So place a priority on relationships.

As a catechist, who you are and how you treat others echoes Jesus' way and words, or blocks them out. When you act with care, consideration, respect and personal integrity, you make it possible for yourself, your students and those you work with to grow, learn, become more successful, more caring, and more faithful—a win/win situation.

(5) Seek first to understand, then to be understood. To enable and empower all involved in your catechetical ministry to

win hinges on understanding those you teach and work with. The key is to learn to listen with your heart and eyes as well as with your ears—to listen in order to understand. We tend to judge, interpret, give advice and teach from our own perceptions of others and their needs rather than to listen carefully to what they say and do, and to the feelings their words, gestures and actions reveal.

Once you understand others, then you and your message will more readily be understood and accepted.

(6) Synergize. Synergy means that people working creatively together achieve more than they could accomplish separately. Learning and teaching together generates enthusiasm, self-respect, pride, and greater wisdom than each one possesses. And it is not boring!

Learn to value the gifts and differences in others, taking seriously—as colearners, coteachers, cocreators, cocatechists—those you teach and work with.

Explore ways to draw out the special gifts of each. Plan lessons together with other catechists, and even with those you teach. Use cooperative learning and other ways of involving you and your students in learning and teaching together.

(7) Sharpen the saw. Take time to renew yourself and your ministry. Find ways to replenish your energy and enthusiasm. Continue learning about catechesis and related topics. Read catechetical magazines, attend occasional conferences, listen to audiotapes, view videos.

Even more important, develop your relationship with Christ. Pray regularly in whatever ways you find meaningful. Read the Bible reflectively, prayerfully. Reach out to help people who are hurting. Work for a more just society.

Otherwise you cannot "echo," as a catechist, Christ, His way and His teachings.

You might find Stephen Covey's book a challenging way to reflect more deeply on becoming a more effective catechist.

3.

How Teach Like Jesus?

"I was sitting at the kitchen table preparing my seventh-grade lesson, when for some reason I just started thinking to myself how good it would be for me to teach like Jesus did. But then I wasn't sure just how Jesus taught. How did he?"

That is a fascinating question. Jesus certainly was a master teacher, but just how did he teach?

The Gospels provide our chief clues and, while they are not biographies of Jesus, they do let us see glimpses of Jesus' ways of teaching. Let's try to sketch them.

(1) Jesus taught mainly by example. People learned Jesus' message most convincingly by watching him, getting to know him, observing how he lived, how he treated people, how he prayed, how he observed God's law.

We teach most effectively the same way. Our students learn of God and Jesus more by who and how we are than by what we say. A thought-provoking banner put it well: "You are the Christ others know best!"

(2) Jesus spoke with authority. Unlike the other Jewish teachers of his time, Jesus spoke with a unique authority. He not only quoted God's Word, He was—and is—God's Word.

Our catechetical ministry is to echo God's Word. Our true authority as catechists comes from our own openness to God's Word, Jesus Christ, and our faithful response, clearly evident in our lives.

(3) Jesus taught by speaking to people's experiences. Jesus walked with people along life's journey, sharing their experiences, sensing their joys and sorrows, responding to their

8

needs and desires—a greedy but guilt-filled Zacchaeus, an adulterous woman, blind Bartimaeus, fearful but honest Nicodemus, a paralyzed man, a rich young man.

We need to do the same by getting to know our students as best we can, tailoring our teaching to their experiences, abilities, needs, desires and learning styles.

(4) Jesus taught by asking questions. The Gospels record some of Jesus' questions, questions that open up the underlying mystery of life and the human heart. "Who do you say that I am?" "What are you looking for?" "What profit would there be for one to gain the whole world and forfeit his life?"

We can learn to ask questions like Jesus, questions that probe below the surface of daily experiences, that open the mind to critical reflection, the heart to pondering, and our hands to sharing.

(5) Jesus taught by telling stories. Jesus rarely spoke in abstractions. He taught the most profound truths through stories. We know them as parables and they still speak to us— Good Samaritan, Prodigal Son, Unjust Steward, Sower and Seed, Rich Man and Lazarus.

We need to work at improving our storytelling skills and finding good, relevant stories—in newspapers and magazines, children's literature, films, videos and TV.

(6) Jesus taught by using images. Jesus' teaching is filled with imagery. He speaks to the heart and mind through the imagination and senses, with word-pictures—a woman sweeping her house in search of a lost coin, a dog licking a poor beggar's sores, a farmer sowing seed, birds soaring freely above beautiful flowers, a final wedding banquet, new wine and old wineskins. We catechists can learn from him to use concrete, poetic language, colorful images, photos, art, music, video, TV, to stir the religious imaginations of our students.

(7) Jesus taught with loving honesty. Jesus pierced right to the heart, to the truth of things, whether it was comforting or

disconcerting, reassuring or challenging. But he always did so with compassion, understanding and love.

Here we may find it harder to teach as Jesus did. We live in a very undemanding culture in which we rarely challenge ourselves or our young with the hard sides of truth and love. We need to teach honestly, strongly, yet always with care.

(8) Jesus' teaching always invited a response. Jesus did not teach just for the sake of sharing information or ideas. He always expected a practical, life-changing response. His teaching was always a call, an invitation, a challenge not only to hear God's Word but to live it.

We catechists are called to do the same. We do need to teach basic truths, Church teachings, moral principles, but we do so not just to inform the mind but to move the will and change the heart. Third World catechists speak of "orthopraxis" (right living) as well as "orthodoxy" (right beliefs).

(9) A story summary of how Jesus taught: Luke 24:31-35. Perhaps one story in Luke's Gospel sums up how Jesus taught. Read and reread Luke 24:31-35. Meditate on it. Watch Jesus walk with the two disciples, sense their pain and confusion, ask them about it, listen as they tell their stories, only then draw on biblical stories about himself that speak to their stories, and accept their invitation to share a meal. In the process their hearts found new hope and joy, they recognized the risen Lord at their table and on their journey, and they changed their lives, returning to the community of disciples and taking up its mission to share the Good News.

Your question is a reminder to us all to try to teach as Jesus did.

4.

What Can We Hope to Accomplish?

"I teach fifth grade. Our textbook deals with the seven sacraments. I think I do a good job of explaining to my class the meaning of the sacraments. But an article I read recently says catechists are to teach 'love' and lead their students to 'conversion experiences.' Now I'm confused and frustrated. What am I supposed to be doing?"

We understand your frustrations and will try to clarify the question of catechists' objectives. We find it helpful to shift our focus from ourselves as teachers to our students as learners. That means thinking less of "what I'm supposed to teach or do" than of "what I want them to learn."

That places the question of our objectives in terms of our students' *learning outcomes.*

Learning Outcomes

By "learning outcomes" educators simply mean, "what we want those we teach to learn." Generally speaking, there are three kinds of learning outcomes:
• *cognitive* (e.g., knowledge, understanding, reasoning skills)
• *affective* (e.g., feelings, attitudes, valuing)
• *behavioral* or *life-style* (decision, actions, habits).

Your question points to all three kinds of learning outcomes: "the meaning of the sacraments" (cognitive), "love" (affective), and "conversion experiences" (behavioral/life-style).

As catechists we need to plan and to teach for all three of these important learning outcomes. All of these are needed to help out students' *"faith* become living, conscious, and active," which is the goal of catechesis, according to the Vatican II (*Bishops*, 14).

Cognitive Outcomes

Typically we catechists tend to give greatest attention to *cognitive* learning outcomes. You mention that your fifth-graders learn well the meaning of the seven sacraments. We will use your example of sacramental catechesis to illustrate the three kinds of learning outcomes.

Regarding the sacraments, it is important for Catholics to have some *knowledge* of the sacramental symbols and their meanings. It is important, too, to know some of the biblical stories that lie behind the sacramental symbolism. Knowing the Church's teachings about the sacraments is also important.

Catholic theologians affirm that *knowing* such *facts, stories,* and *beliefs* is one of the major components of Christian faith. They call it simply: *believing.*

Affective Outcomes

Yet daily experience makes it clear that Catholics, young or old, may know much about the sacraments without appreciating them. Their heads may be full of religious knowledge but their hearts have not been touched by it.

So religious educators stress *affective* learning outcomes as well. These are experienced in the "heart" and affect our basic values. In terms of the sacraments, they include *feelings*, like reverence and awe for the Church's sacraments, a deep *appreciation* of them as personally valuable, a *desire* to participate more fully in their celebration, a *sense of wonder* at the mystery of God's loving presence through common material objects and human gestures. Theologians point out that such *affective* outcomes are a second and more vital part of Christian faith. They call it *trusting.*

Behavioral Outcomes

Ultimately, catechesis is meant to impact not just one's knowledge and emotions but also one's life-style. Catechesis has to do with *living* as a Catholic, a Christian, a disciple of Jesus. *Behavioral* or *life-style* learning objectives are of utmost importance for catechists. In our example of sacramental catechesis, we want those we teach to *celebrate* the Church's sacraments, and to *live* sacramental lives—aware of God's gracious presence with them always and everywhere, and responsive to God's call to accept God's love and share it with others, especially those in most need.

"*Behavioral*" or "*life-style*" learning outcomes move beyond *head* and *heart* to engage *hands and feet.*

Theologians stress that a third essential part of faith is *doing.* Without "works," without expressing love of God and others, head-faith and heart-faith remain dead and unfruitful.

True Priorities

While recognizing our own limitations and the very real limitations of time and place, we catechists need to keep in mind all three kinds of learning outcomes as objectives. By our teaching styles and skills we will want to work to enable all three learning outcomes.

Of these three general objectives, the most important are the life-style or *behavioral* outcomes ("doing"). Second in importance are the *affective* ("trusting"). In third place come the *cognitive* outcomes ("believing"). As Jesus puts it: "Blessed are those who hear the word of God and observe it" (Lk 11:28).

We hope our discussion of objectives clears up some of your confusion about what you are doing. We are aware, too, that it may raise new questions and challenges.

5.

Where Are We Headed?

"I've been teaching religion for almost 20 years. So many things have changed in religious education during those years. Is there any way to guess what changes are coming in the next few years? Where do you think we are headed in religious education?"

We are certainly not experts at predicting the future, but we do see five or six major trends in the world at large and in the Church that are increasingly affecting contemporary catechesis, mostly, we believe, for the better.

Community

One of the strongest trends in our "high-tech," complex society is for "high-touch" *communities* in which people can be known by name and actually make a difference in one another's lives. At its best, the pull to smaller, more intimate communities tends also to raise consciousness of and participation in the broader, multicultural, global society and Church.

This dual pull toward small-group intimacy and global consciousness is evident in "base Christian communities," both in the Third World and in our own country. The R.C.I.A., Children's Catechumenate, Renew, family-centered catechesis, and youth ministry are some of the more obvious examples of this trend to community in contemporary catechesis. And individual catechists seem more consciously to foster a sense of community in their classes.

Justice and Peace

A second trend, directly related to the first, is the growing commitment to *compassion, social justice and world peace.* The tearing down of the Berlin Wall, the dramatic developments in Eastern Europe, and worldwide revulsion at Chinese, Romanian, Salvadoran, Bosnian, Serbian and Somalian atrocities symbolize a global shift toward a more just and nonviolent world rooted in respect for human rights.

In many parts of the world the Catholic Church—through bold pastorals and often heroic personal witness—has been in the vanguard of this broad movement toward compassion, justice and peace.

Catechetical guidelines, textbooks and individual catechists increasingly raise social consciousness and invite participation in social action. Besides encouraging compassion for suffering individuals, catechesis tends more and more to invite social analysis and actions to change unjust structures that cause so much human suffering by violating people's rights.

Concern for social justice increasingly embraces animal rights, environmental protection, and the equitable use of natural resources.

Spirituality

A third trend arises from the gnawing search for happiness and meaning in a complex, changing, consumerist, often unjust society. We experience and observe an insistent need for a deeper *spirituality.*

People long for roots, for values, for meaning, for ways of experiencing God, for ways to pray, for ways to cope with life's challenges and to respond to life's opportunities. Catechesis more and more stresses personal commitment and relationship with Jesus Christ as the source of meaning and the guide to a satisfying way of life.

Imagination

A fourth trend is a growing respect for *imagination.* The power of the imagination in creating community, inspiring compassion and justice, and providing meaning and purpose to millions is evident, for example, in words like "solidarity" and *glasnost,* in symbols like the Berlin Wall, in heroes like Walesa, Mandela, Romero, Sakharov, and Mother Teresa. Catechists increasingly recognize the power of the religious imagination expressed in symbols, rituals, music, popular devotions and saints. For most of the Church's history, catechesis drew consciously on the rich treasures of Judeo-Christian imagination. Today we are rediscovering the vital role of the religious imagination in catechesis.

Literacy

And finally, a fifth trend found in secular education as well as religious education is a concern for critical reflection and *literacy.* "Back to the basics" and "cultural literacy" find an echo in a felt need for "Catholic literacy." Catechists are increasingly aware of the need to give more att ntion to basic beliefs, prayers and practices. The *Catechism of the Catholic Church* shows the Vatican's concern about basic beliefs. Greater attention to basic factual knowledge needs to be balanced with critical reflection and honest questioning.

This healthy conservative movement has one serious danger, that it may ignore or reject the valuable advances in catechesis since Vatican II—respect for God's Word spoken in the "signs of the times," or daily experience, and the current trends mentioned above.

To us these five trends are major indicators of where catechesis may be moving as we enter the final decade of the 20th-century.

6.

What Are Alternative Catechetical Models?

"I've been teaching religion for eight years, six in a parochial school, and the last two in CCD. With each passing year, I question more whether a classroom is the best place to help children learn what it means to be a Catholic. Does anyone else feel the same way?"

Yours is a question we hear more and more often recently, usually in terms of "alternative models" of religious education.

For the past 400 years, the dominant approach to catechesis/religious education has been a *school* model—all week or once-a-week, with teachers, students (mostly children), classrooms, textbooks, lesson plans, and tests.

This *school* or *educational* model of catechesis has helped generations of Catholics learn basic beliefs, prayers, and moral principles. It remains valuable through the competent efforts of thousands of dedicated teachers, administrators and parents.

So Why Other Models?

Yet like yourself, others have been feeling a need for different approaches. We know that faith is more than intellectual knowledge of Church teachings and practices. Faith has more to do with the heart, with commitment, values, and life-style. Catechists increasingly ask whether an *educational/school* model alone can achieve all that.

During the first 1500 years of the Church's history, there were no Catholic schools or once-a-week religion classes as we know them. Catholics learned in other ways what to believe, how to pray, and how to live—namely in the *family*, at *home*, at *Sunday*

17

worship in their local *parish church*, with its *statues, stained glass,* and *beautiful music,* through *popular devotions, feast days, holy-days,* and from the all-pervasive *Catholic culture.*

Drawing on this rich tradition and recent experiments, the *National Catechetical Directory* proposes a surprising number of models in addition to the *educational/school model* (#225-231). In fact the *NCD* asserts that "every pastoral activity has a catechetical dimension" (#39). Catechists, liturgists, and other pastoral ministers are now developing these exciting models of initiation and faith formation.

What Other Models?

All the "alternative" models are *pastoral* rather than *in-structional,* centering in *family, community, parish,* and *liturgy,* rather than in *school* or *classroom.* These are some of the important current *pastoral/community* models:

• *Small groups,* that gather within a parish for study, prayer, spiritual growth, family enrichment, and/or social justice. Most challenging are *Small Christian Communities* or *comunidades eclesiales de base,* in which a number of families share their lives and faith more totally.

• *Family-centered catechesis,* which organizes religious education around the family, takes place in homes with parents as catechists. This model tends to be *intergenerational,* with children of varying ages, parents, and even grandparents focusing on the same theme each week.

• *Brief intensive experiences.* Youth weekends, Cursillo, retreats, and other brief but intense faith experiences have been very effective for conversion and faith growth. So, too, has *Vacation Bible School*—one or two weeks of enjoyable, active learning, prayer and fun during summer vacation.

• *Liturgy of the Word.* Children separate from the adult community during the Liturgy of the Word each Sunday so that both groups may experience and respond to God's Word more meaningfully.

• *Lectionary-based catechesis.* Ritually-oriented catechesis centers on the official Church *Lectionary* of biblical readings and prayers for the Sunday Eucharist rather than on textbooks arranged around doctrinal and moral themes.

• *Catechumenate—adults, children.* The *Rite of Christian Initiation of Adults* (RCIA) provides a community and liturgy-based model of catechesis for adult converts, and suggests a similar approach for children—both involving the whole parish.

What About Alternative Models?

We appreciate these models, old and new, but feel that the term "alternative" is unfortunate. It too easily leads many to infer that the *pastoral/community* models should replace the *education/school* models. Actually both are valuable for catechesis today. We prefer to speak of *"complementary"* models.

We also believe parishes normally need a balance of several of these models because catechesis embraces *education, formation* and *initiation* (*NCD*, 39). The "ritual catechesis" of the RCIA, or of the Children's Catechumenate, for example, cannot alone provide adequate instruction in Catholic beliefs, history, and traditions.

Each model has its own strengths and limitations. A sound catechetical plan carefully balances selected *educational/school* and *pastoral/community* models.

Lastly, we believe that we all need to avoid exaggerated claims for any one model as the "only" valid approach to catechesis today.

So, you are not alone in your search for "complementary" models.

7.

Catholic Literacy? What? Why?

"Our pastor recently complained in a homily that we've lost our 'Catholic literacy' because of recent religious education fads. Maybe I'm part of the problem because I've been teaching religion for almost a dozen years. I keep worrying about what 'Catholic literacy' is and what I can do about it, if anything."

Your pastor is touching on an important current trend in the Church, one that can become very creative or very destructive.

The term, "Catholic literacy" (related to the growing concern in our country about "cultural literacy") refers to "what Catholics need to know."

Disturbed by studies showing Catholic youth weak in knowledge of Catholic beliefs, prayers, history, traditions, and saints, many Catholics see a need to stress knowledge of such basic facts in religious education. They call for a renewal of "Catholic literacy."

Catholic Literacy

Understood in this way, "Catholic literacy" is obviously important. Your pastor rightly bemoans its weakening in the Church today. Knowledge of basic Catholic beliefs, prayers, and moral principles—clearly set forth in the *National Catechetical Directory*—is vital for at least four reasons:

(1) Catholic Identity. In a pluralistic world such as ours, a sense of one's religious identity is critical. Part of knowing who one is as a Catholic involves knowing basic facts about Catholic belief, worship, and life-style.

(2) Catholic Language. The Church is a worldwide network of communities. To be able to communicate with other Catholics in a parish or in the global Church requires a kind of common language. Just as family members share a common language grounded in family experiences and traditions, Catholics have a similar language.

(3) Catholic Wisdom. In a changing, complex, confusing world we need some source of wisdom to help us interpret our experiences. Drawing on well over 20 centuries of Judeo-Christian experience, we Catholics possess a priceless treasure of wisdom about life's meaning and purpose to help us make sense out of and cope with life's challenges and opportunities. Our Catholic young people have a right to share in this wisdom.

(4) Catholic Images. The central images of our faith tradition also provide invaluable keys to shaping the future. Catholic images drawn from the Bible, symbolized in the liturgy, and enfleshed in the lives of great Christian women and men, have the power to stir our hearts and direct our minds to transform ourselves and the world.

Cautions

Granting the importance of "Catholic literacy," we need to express a strong word of caution about contemporary efforts to restore such basic knowledge in religious education.

It is deceptive to expect increased "Catholic literacy" to insure growth in Catholic faith. The fallacy is to identify faith growth with increased information about Catholic faith. Faith is much more a matter of affectivity (trust, surrender, love) and life-style (compassion, justice, prayer) than conceptual knowledge (basic truths). True faith is caught much more than taught, and can be taught primarily through affective and experiential methods—the very activities typically criticized by overly enthusiastic advocates of Catholic literacy.

Practical Tips

So what can you do to foster Catholic literacy?

(1) Become more literate. Keep expanding your knowledge and appreciation of the riches of our Catholic heritage. Become more familiar with contemporary Catholic trends. Read regularly, particularly in the area of Catholic faith that you are teaching. Become familiar with the Vatican's recent *Catechism of the Catholic Church.*

(2) Stress Literacy. Most religion textbooks today give considerable attention to Catholic beliefs, practices, history, traditions, prayers, heroes and heroines. Work conscientiously to help your students learn these Catholic basics.

(3) Be Creative. Engage your students' religious imaginations by creative activities that may touch their emotions and involve them in living out what they profess. For example, use sacred art and music, poetry and story, images and symbols, lives of saints and other great Christians, field trips and service projects. In this way balance the stress on conceptual literacy with the nurturing of personal faith that shows itself in love and justice.

(4) Be Caring. Ultimately the most important thing you, as catechist, can do to help those you teach become more authentically Catholic is to care about them, love them, treat them with respect, honesty and compassion. Let them see in you what it means to be Catholic.

We hope this is helpful. You might talk over these ideas with your pastor, thereby sharing your mutual concern for Catholic literacy.

8.

What Does a Good Class Look Like?

"As my first class of a new year of teaching gets closer, what I think I need are some guidelines to help me start off on the right foot. I'd like some clues as to what makes for good classes—to help me picture what good classes look like."

While good classes may look quite different on the surface, they usually reveal common underlying characteristics. We will list what we consider *10 indicators* of good religious education classes.

(1) Inviting. The physical and social environment of successful classes tends to be inviting, attractive, comfortable, hospitable. Catechists foster this in many ways—being well-prepared, welcoming students as they arrive, being available before and after class, quickly learning names, displaying meaningful, eye-catching posters, banners, photos, art, and students' work, decorating with flowers, playing music, rearranging the furniture.

(2) Interesting. Good religion classes are interesting. They stimulate learning by relating biblical, liturgical and doctrinal content to the learners' needs, experiences and questions.

To get to know those they teach, good catechists observe how students act, spend time chatting with them, listen carefully to what they say, study their writing and other creative work, listen to music they like, and read stories written for people their age.

(3) Interactive. Good religion classes usually have a lot of interaction among students and between students and their catechist. Instead of a one-way flow of talk or ideas, everyone is actively engaged in the teaching/learning process—listening, reflecting, talking, writing, drawing, discussing, praying, making things.

(4) Inquiring. Good catechetical classes are full of questioning, exploring, probing—"faith seeking understanding."

Good catechists encourage students to question, to take risks, to learn from mistakes. They create a thoughtful, reflective atmosphere, use "open questions" that stimulate deeper thinking more than "closed questions" that simply seek information, and reward good questions as much as correct answers.

(5) Integrated. A good religious education class relates to what is going on in the life of the Church and world at large. Catechesis integrates human experiences and world events with the Bible, Church worship, Church teachings, and the example of exemplary Christians.

Wherever possible, good catechists draw on the secular and religious news media, parish bulletins, neighborhood newsletters, relevant social, political, economic, cultural and religious events. God's Word may be heard anywhere.

(6) Collaborative. Good catechetical classes exhibit much cooperative or collaborative learning. Students work together in small teams during at least part of each session. Collaborative work draws out the unique gifts of each and makes it possible for students to share those gifts, thereby helping one another learn. Working together can foster a greater sense of responsibility and of community.

(7) Creative. Good classes typically are creative classes. Creative catechists use various media to engage the differing learning styles of both teacher and learners alike. Activities draw on imagination and mind, nonverbal and verbal, feelings and ideas. Art, story, poetry, video, music, drama, role-playing,

writing, drawing, painting and crafts touch head and heart through the senses. Creative catechists also tap the talents of parents and other adults.

(8) Enjoyable. Good catechesis involves joy, which suggests delight, pleasure, fun. Enjoyment is the oil of learning, making learning easier, smoother. Fun is normally a positive factor in learning, more so perhaps today.

Good catechists, on occasion, make use of games, cartoons, song, movement, drama and humor. Spontaneous laughter is common. Enjoyable classes are purposeful yet playful, demanding and delightful.

(9) Caring. Good classes reveal genuine caring. Participants show mutual respect by listening to one another, trying to understand, refusing to put others down, and cooperating. Caring classes are marked by courtesy, sensitivity and compassion, appreciation and praise, gentleness and reverence. Catechists and students may become companions and friends as well as colearners.

(10) Prayerful. Prayer is a vital part of good catechetical classes, since a major purpose of catechesis is to help people learn how to pray.

Good catechists carefully plan various kinds of prayer into their sessions—always related to what they are teaching. They draw on the rich Catholic prayer tradition, which includes prayer forms like vocal prayer, bodily prayer, silent meditation, spontaneous prayer, litanies, mantras, traditional prayers, and liturgical prayers.

Those are our *10 indicators* of good catechetical/religious education classes. We hope they help you picture what a good class looks like.

9.

How Help Children Grow Spirituality?

"Recently one of my third-graders insisted that God didn't create us out of nothing, but rather made us out of love. I've been thinking about that ever since. How could a 9-year-old have such a profound insight? Is she unusually spiritual? Can I, a catechist, help all those I teach to grow spiritually?"

Youngsters at times come up with the most amazing insights into what life is really all about. We adults easily forget that children can have deep spiritual lives.

Children's Spirituality

Harvard psychiatrist, Dr. Robert Coles, has spent all his adult life working with and learning from children. In his recent book, *The Spiritual Life of Children* (Houghton Mifflin, 1990), he shows how the spirituality of children expresses itself in their struggle to make sense of life's journey.

They—like we adults—wonder and ponder questions like, "What is life all about anyway?" "Why am I here?" "Where am I going?" "Why am I the way I am?" "What makes people happy?" "Why is there so much pain?" "What happens after we die?"

Perhaps more quickly than adults the young find their life-pondering leading them to sense a mysterious, mighty, fascinating Presence within the daily mysteries of living. They sense that we are caught up in the embrace of One greater than ourselves and the universe. Depending on their religious heritage, they may name that Presence "God," "Great Spirit," "Allah," "Jehovah"—or find no name satisfying.

Children's deep sense of life's mysterious and alluring Presence tends to overflow into how they try to live, or at least, would like to be able to live.

Catechists' Challenge

Our challenge as catechists is to nurture that innate spirituality within the Catholic tradition. We have the privilege of helping children relate their individual struggles for meaning and purpose to the accumulated wisdom of millions of Christians over 20 centuries—as well as to the varied insights of other fellow-searchers worldwide.

That privileged challenge is two-fold. First, we need to help those we catechize get in touch with their own spirituality. Second, we need to help them enrich their spiritual capacities through the riches of our Catholic tradition.

Learning from Jesus

Interestingly, Robert Coles' fascinating research into the spiritual lives of children echoes the approach reflected in Jesus' Easter journey to Emmaus (Luke 24:13-35).

From both Jesus and Dr. Coles we can learn some helpful hints:

(1) Share their journey. Jesus walked with the two disciples on their troubled journey back home. Dr. Coles spent months, even years, with individual children.

Taking time to enter into an ongoing relationship with those we teach is the key to unlocking a child's inner, spiritual world. As Coles puts it, we need to develop the "capacity to spend time with children in such a way that they want to talk" of their inner wrestling with life's meaning.

(2) Ask questions. Given that growing bond, we can help them by asking real questions about life and/or their Catholic faith tradition, with an honest expectation that they have some-

thing valuable to say in response. The questions may take many forms—simple questions, scenarios or cases, dilemmas, open-ended stories, for example. They may be asked verbally or through photos, video, art, or other media.

Invite the children to respond to the questions however they wish—in words, written or spoken, in drawings or paintings, in gesture.

(3) Listen. As they respond, listen carefully—with your eyes and heart as well as your ears. Sometimes their pictures or body-language say more about their spiritual search than their words.

(4) Tell them the Catholic story. As part of your joint journey share with them Bible stories, liturgical rituals, doctrinal or moral teachings, or saints' lives, that relate to their experiences.

A child can then bounce his or her personal pondering against the Church's spiritual wisdom. If the two mesh, the children may find their Catholic faith tradition meaningful, even exciting and inspiring. If not, they may stifle or redirect their spiritual quest.

(5) Pray with them. Pray with the children at some points during this process. The rich spiritual tradition of the Church allows for a wide variety of prayer forms—traditional prayers like the Our Father, psalms, spontaneous prayer, silent meditation, bodily gesture, art, music or song, dance. What is vital is that the "Catholic" prayer resonates with the children's own prayers.

(6) Live out with them what you and they are coming to grasp. Your example can be a concrete model of living out the spirituality you are helping them get in touch with. The children also need opportunities to translate—through practical projects—their emerging spiritual insights into the way to live.

As you become more sensitive and skilled in nurturing children's spiritual search, you will discover that your insightful third-grader is less unusual than you now suspect.

10.

How Teach to Touch Hearts and Lives?

"I sometimes wonder if I'm not wasting my time teaching religion. So little of what I teach seems to make much difference in the lives of my students. They do well on my tests but I keep wondering if what they learn in my classes touches them at all. Or is that too much to ask? Maybe I expect too much."

Yours is a very common and practical question. We've asked it of ourselves.

Aside from recognizing that we are competing with other powerful forces influencing those we teach—e.g., family, peers, social pressures, advertising, television and music—we also might well look at *how* we are teaching.

For example, skilled at informing your students' minds (as your tests verify), you may not be using teaching methods designed to touch their hearts and impact their life-style. You are not alone in this.

Methods Affect Outcomes

How we teach directly relates to *what* our students learn. That is, the *methods* we use in our classes govern the kind of *learning outcomes* we can realistically expect.

So we need to ask ourselves if our methodology matches what we hope to happen.

In preparing a class we should:

(1), *decide what our main goal is—cognitive* (head), *affective* (heart), *or behavioral* (life-style), *and then*

29

(2) *select methods that can work toward that goal.*

This can be challenging. It may mean learning and practicing new kinds of teaching skills. But the task is well worth the effort.

Cognitive Methods

Most of us tend to be more comfortable with teaching methods aimed at imparting information, explaining ideas, encouraging critical thinking. We talk, lecture, explain, ask questions and expect answers, help children learn facts and ideas, have students read and write, do research, make charts, timelines, maps, do puzzles.

These methods work for teaching knowledge and understanding of the bible, doctrinal teachings, moral principles, liturgical rituals, and Church history.

Affective Methods

Different methods are needed to touch the heart, affect attitudes, and influence values. For that we need to use more *affective* methods and skills. These are much more *personal, imaginative, poetic and creative.*

Most important of all is *how you are* with the students. This creates a *learning environment* that affects all that goes on in your classes and in your students' learning. Are you excited about your faith? Do you smile a lot? Are you glad to be with your students? Do you affirm them? Do you accept their weaknesses while challenging them to grow? Do you honestly try to understand them? Do you listen to their questions, dreams, hurts? Do you trust them? Do you really pray with them?

Secondly, look at the *place* where you teach. Does it convey warmth, welcome, respect, love? Is it a place of beauty, peace, and joy?

Thirdly, look at your *methods.* To touch hearts, change attitudes, influence values, you need to stir *feelings* through your students' *senses* and *imaginations.* Story and poetry and children's literature do this in a way even the best of explanations cannot. So can reflective and creative writing, journaling, and diary keeping. Honest dialogue and discussion may also impact attitudes and values.

So, too, may the lives of great Christian women and men.

Nonverbal methods—like gestures, body-language, music, photos, film, video, drawing or painting—are often more powerful than words in touching the heart.

Behavioral Methods

If we hope for some change in our students' actions and life-style, we need to use experiential methods. As Liza Doolittle in *My Fair Lady* put it, "Words, words, words. Show me!"

Such methods center on *experience,* the more direct, personal, and engaging the better.

Most effective are *real-life projects* like working in a soup-kitchen, visiting sick or elderly persons, writing letters to public officials, taking part in a demonstration, designing and participating in a prayer experience, the Eucharist, or weekend retreat.

Where real-life experiential projects are not possible, *alternative* or *simulated* experiences are useful. Role-playing and dramatizing can be effective. So can the creation of a film, filmstrip or video. Simulation games can be purchased or made up that involve students in real-life issues and experiments.

What is important is that the students are actively, experientially engaged in doing something related to their lives and their faith. So, don't give up. You are making a difference! Expanding and adapting your teaching skills along affective and experiential lines may let you make an even bigger difference in your students' lives.

11.

How Improve Your Skills?

"I've been a catechist for three years. My classes are generally good and I love the children. My textbook is so good I don't need to spend much time planning. But I don't feel I'm getting any better as a teacher. How can I sharpen my skills as a catechist?"

While we reflected on your excellent question, a seemingly unrelated incident came to mind. Perhaps it suggests an answer.

One day a famous architect stood admiring the awesome beauty of a medieval cathedral. After several moments of silence, he observed quietly: *"God lies in the details."*

Perhaps that is the key to honing your catechetical skills: *more careful attention to details* in planning.

Visualizing

We find it helpful to play out an upcoming class in our minds. We try to visualize just how it will unfold. *Previsualization* forces us to focus on concrete details, rather than to remain with a rather vague sense of what we hope to accomplish.

As we imagine, step by step, how we want our class to flow, we become conscious of details related to the *who, what, when, where, how* and *why* of the lesson development.

Careful attention to these details can make all the difference—and will soon become second nature.

Who?

We all need to develop a more detailed sense of who we are as catechists—our feelings, our knowledge, our teaching style, our skills, or limitations. Build consciously on your gifts, while finding ways to compensate for and overcome your weaknesses.

Vital, too, is knowing more and more about those you teach—their backgrounds, families, abilities, likes and dislikes, feelings and learning styles.

Then plan accordingly. Who will read the Bible story? Who will lead a song, play the guitar? Who needs special attention? Who will run the video or stereo? Who will lead the discussion?

What?

The "what" refers first to the *content* of the class. Often we remain overly vague about the meaning of a Bible text, a liturgical symbol, ritual, or church teaching.

Pay attention, for example, to details of a Bible story: its context, author, purpose, images and language, original meaning. What does it mean today? What does it mean to you? What can it mean to those you are teaching?

The "what" also relates to details regarding the *resources* you plan to use. What materials seem best—paper and pencils, crayons, or paints? What photos or art might help? What film or video need I order? What equipment will I need? What needs to be duplicated?

Where?

We often take for granted the place where we have our classes. Yet attention to detail in making it an attractive *environment* for learning can greatly affect our lessons. Sometimes a photo, art work, poster, flowers, or music can make all the difference. How you arrange the room, make use of light and darkness, audio and visual stimuli, situate boys, girls, friends, can help or hinder student interest and learning. A lesson in a home—or outside, in church, in the library—will be different from the same lesson in a classroom. Sometimes a fieldtrip to a museum, soup kitchen, synagogue or cemetery will make a lesson come alive.

When?

Often *timing* is a most critical detail. What day or time of day you have class can make a big difference. When you introduce prayer in a lesson may make the prayer meaningful or simply rote. Is there a rhythm to your class, with enough variety, changes of pace, to keep up interest? How much time to give to each part of the lesson so it isn't overly rushed or boringly long?

How?

There are often several ways of accomplishing something—each with its unique effect. How will I share this Bible story—read it? tell it in my own words? show a film of it? use sacred art? listen to a Gospel song? act it out? draw it? make a movie of it? How will I prepare for it? introduce it? guide it? follow up on it?

Details of "how" get into the nitty-gritty that can make or break a class: How will I read a story if I have the lights out for effect? How many extensions will I need to use a TV and VCR in this room? How run the slide projector?

Why?

Sometimes the hardest area to focus on details is that of goals or objectives. We tend to be vague. We need to remain flexible. Yet we also have to be as clear and precise as possible regarding our *objectives* in each class and in each activity.

Exactly why are we doing this activity? Why do this after that? Why dramatize rather than read a parable? Why pray in the middle of class rather than at the end?

Details

More careful attention to details is our suggestion for improving your catechetical skills.

It may not seem all that exciting, but as the famous architect wisely perceived: "God lies in the details!"

12.

What Are Some Good Bible Aids?

*"I really like the way our textbook uses stories and
prayers from the Bible. Sometimes I'd like to find out
more about some of the quotes, or I want to find a
good text for a lesson or prayer service. Where can I
find information like that?"*

Your question is one we often hear. Fortunately there are a
number of excellent resources available. Here are some old
standbys and some exciting new publications.

Bibles: Study Editions

Perhaps most useful is a "study edition," or "Catholic study
edition" of the Bible you use regularly. These editions are filled
with introductions to biblical books, maps, time-lines, notes explaining chapters, verses, words, and cross-references to related
passages throughout the Bible.

We would recommend a "study edition" of the *New American Bible,* with *Revised New Testament* (1986) and *Revised
Book of Psalms* (1991). It is the translation used in most American parishes on Sundays.

However, you might look at and prefer one of these fine
translations: the *New Revised Standard Version* (1990)—uses in-
clusive language, is the choice of mainline Protestant Churches
and is approved for use in Catholic worship; the *New Jerusalem
Bible* (1985) with its excellent notes and references is widely
used by British and American Catholics; the *Good News Bible,*
officially *Today's English Version* (1979) in more modern, col-
loquial English is often preferred for use with youth; and, the

Christian Community Bible (1988), reveals the Bible as seen through the eyes of Third World poor.

For hints on getting the most out of such Bibles, you might find helpful the chapter, "How Can We Get Into The Bible?" in our book, *How to be a Better Catechist* (1989).

Commentaries

In addition to a sound "study edition" of the Bible, you would do well to own or have easy access to a Bible commentary.

Biblical commentaries normally provide in-depth background on the Bible's origins, authors, themes and special problems, introductions to individual books, and verse-by-verse interpretations.

We recommend *The Collegeville Bible Commentary* (1989). It is available as separate booklets for individual biblical books. Each booklet contains the text of the biblical book as well as the commentary, and may be purchased separately. A one volume edition (without Bible text) covers the entire Bible.

You might also consider *The New Jerome Biblical Commentary* (1990). It provides more scholarly and detailed commentary on the entire Bible (without biblical text).

Additional resources, like the following, may further increase your competence. Check your parish library.

Concordances

If you need to find a particular quotation or story for a class or prayer service, turn to a concordance. Knowing just one word of the passage allows you to find it.

Nelson's Complete Concordance of the New American Bible (1977) lists every time a word is used in the *New American* Bible. Under the one word you know you will find the particular quote or story you seek.

Similar complete or abbreviated concordances are available for most other translations.

If you are into computers, you might look at one of the new software concordances, like *QuickVerse 2.0* (in the translation you choose), from Parsons Technology (1990). It makes your search easier and faster.

Biblical Dictionaries

A biblical dictionary can help you learn more about a person (Zacchaeus), group (Pharisees), place (Jericho), feast (Passover), ritual (baptism), thing (manna), theme (covenant), belief (creation), or other biblical fact.

Our long-time favorite, recently reprinted, is the *Dictionary of the Bible,* by John L. McKenzie, S.J. (1967). Smaller, but also useful, is Dr. Donald M. McFarlan's *Concise Bible Dictionary* (1986).

Another old favorite is Xavier Leon-Dufour's *Dictionary of Biblical Theology* (1973). It is a rich source for tracing key themes that run through the entire Bible, like "love," "redemption," or "sin."

Atlases

At times you may want to have a clearer idea of where certain biblical events, like the Exodus, took place. For that a biblical atlas is handy.

We've long used Hammond's *Atlas of the Bible Lands* (1984). There is also the new *Collegeville Bible Study Atlas* (1990), and for computers, the *PC Bible Atlas* from Parsons Technology (1992).

Putting It All Together

A remarkable recent book tries quite successfully to combine something of all the above kinds of helps into one volume. *The Catholic Study Bible* (1990) contains the entire Bible (*New American Bible*—study edition) as well as commentary, dictionary/glossary, and atlas. This one book alone may adequately meet your present needs.

Finally, we recommend another excellent book, *Responses to 101 Questions on the Bible* (1990), by one of the leading biblical scholars, Raymond E. Brown, S.S.. It gives a fine overview of a modern Catholic approach to the Bible.

With helps like these, we catechists can all become more at home with the Bible in our lives and in our teaching.

13.

How Successful Were We?

"We are getting near the end of the school year and I keep wondering how well I did with my class. Besides, our D.R.E. urged us catechists individually to evaluate our year. How do you know you've been a good catechist or not? I'm not even sure what questions to ask myself."

Here are several approaches we find helpful for an evaluation.

Set aside some quiet time for your evaluation. Paper and pencil (or computer) may be helpful. Note down anything you want to remember for next year's teaching.

We begin with three broad, evocative sets of questions.

- How do I feel about the year as a whole?

- What do I feel happiest about, most proud of? What were some of the finer moments? What worked?

- What do I feel worst about? What were some truly weak moments? What didn't work?

These three questions give us an important overview of our perception of the year's classes. Next we move on to more specific questions—about our students, ourselves, and our situation.

Our Students

We first explore indications of our students' *faith-growth* (our overall goal) in terms of objectives we set at the start of the year. Three broad catechetical learning objectives (cognitive, affective, behavioral) relate to the three traditional aspects of Catholic *faith* (believing, trusting, doing).

(1) Cognitive objectives ("believing": knowledge, understanding, reasoning): This is usually the easiest set of questions to answer.

How well have our students learned the intellectual content we set out to share with them?

Clues to answer this question are found in our quizzes, tests, and questioning in class.

What meaning does what they learned have for their daily lives?

How have they grown in the basic skill or process of looking at their lives in the light of their Catholic faith, and vice-versa?

Our students' creative work, their questions, and class discussion provide clues to answering these two questions.

(2) Affective objectives ("trusting": feelings, attitudes, valuing). We ask ourselves questions like:

To what extent did the students seem to grow during the year in feelings, attitudes and values that are part of faith-growth, like:

- *interest*—in learning about their lives and their faith
- *respect*—for themselves, us, other students, the world, the Church
- *trust*—in God, us, one another, the Church
- *caring*—for themselves, for others, for God, for things
- *openness*—to God in their lives, to life's mystery, to people and ideas
- *creativity*
- *compassion* for those in need and a *sense of justice*
- *enjoyment* of religion class.

We find clues to these affective dimensions in our experience and observation of the students.

(3) Behavioral ("doing": decisions, actions, habits): We can at least evaluate our students' actions while they are with us in class, if not during the rest of their lives.

How have the students grown during the year in acting more like followers of Jesus Christ?

We look at behaviors like:

- *participating* responsibly in individual and group activities
- *listening* respectfully to us and one another
- *cooperating* with us, our helpers, and with other students
- *praying* alone and with the class
- *acting more honestly, carefully, compassionately and justly*
- *reaching out* to those in need.

We find clues for answering these questions in the way the students have acted during the year.

Ourselves as Catechists

Next we take a closer look at ourselves as catechists with questions like:

- *What teaching skills am I best at? What skills do I need to work harder on?*
- *What excited me most? What caused me anxiety or frustration?*
- *What did I learn? What knowledge do I most lack?*
- *How did I relate with the students? How much do I really like them and care about them?*

Our Situation

Besides ourselves and our students, other factors greatly affect catechetical experience. We ask ourselves questions about things like these:

- place of class—size of room, room arrangement, feeling created by the environment?

- *time of class*—an up-time or down-time for learning; long enough?

- *textbook we use*—helpful, easy to use, interesting and challenging?

- *other materials and equipment available to us*—pictures, films, videos, posters; recordings, songs, music; projector, cassette player, VCR/TV; craft materials?

- *support we received*—from parents, other catechists, D.R.E. or principal, parish, diocese?

We also find it helpful to ask our students anonymously to write down what they liked best and least about our classes.

We hope we have given you some help toward evaluating your year. Ask your D.R.E. or principal for further guidance in evaluating.

14.

What About Vacation Bible School?

"Our parish is considering having a religious education program during the summer. The Protestant churches in our neighborhood all have Vacation Bible Schools. We are wondering if you think it is a good idea for a Catholic parish. We would appreciate any suggestions."

Actually, summertime catechesis is not new to Catholics. The nationwide CCD program in the United States originated in great part from summer religious education programs in rural parishes in the Northwest and Midwest.

In recent years, more and more Catholic parishes seem to be holding religious education programs during the summer, usually for one or two weeks. The majority of these parishes use the vacation programs as a supplement to their regular school-year programs. Some parishes have replaced once-a-week religious education during the school year with a summer vacation program.

Some Benefits of VCS

Summertime religious education, which we will call Vacation Church School [VCS], has several benefits that are attractive to parishes and families, catechists, children and youth. Here are some we see:

(1) Less pressure. Summer time is often less pressured for everyone involved in religious education. This allows for a more relaxed approach to catechesis. Catechists, parents and

children seem more able to enjoy the religious education experience in summertime.

(2) Much time in a short time frame. Most VCS programs run for one or two weeks. All involved know the time limits and may be motivated to pour their energy more fully into what is a relatively short but intense time frame.

Yet the two weeks of all-morning sessions actually allow for more extended periods of time than in school or CCD, and total more hours than the average year-long CCD program.

(3) Involves new people. In many parishes, parents and teenagers normally not involved in teaching during the year can become actively involved in a short VCS program. Many parents who might feel intimidated by a school-year religion program see ways to bring their gifts to the summer program. Teenagers may be drawn to become involved as catechists, helpers, musicians, or counselors. This can bring a freshness and enthusiasm to the experience, benefiting all concerned, and engaging new people in the parish's ministries.

(4) Fun. Most VCS programs are designed to be fun. While focused on genuine learning and praying, the approaches and methods usually involve more fun, with more music, games, drama, arts and crafts than school or CCD programs. This tends to make for a meaningful, enjoyable catechetical experience.

Some Hints for VCS

To receive these benefits, a parish needs to plan carefully for its VCS program. Here are some hints we have found helpful for carrying out a successful VCS.

(1) Coordinator. Select a capable parishioner as director or coordinator. The VCS coordinator need not be a professional religious educator, administrator, or manager, but someone who deals well with people and has some talent for organizing.

He or she can draw upon the expertise of the parish DRE in selecting materials and training volunteers.

(2) Task leaders. Several persons may be needed to take responsibility for things like recruiting teachers and helpers, advertising the program, overseeing arts and crafts supplies, transportation, refreshments, money, keeping records, and secretarial tasks.

(3) Catechists. It is well worth the time and effort to search for and discover persons in the parish who may or may not be in the school-year religious education program but who have a genuine love for children, are enthusiastic, work well with others, are creative, and have a real willingness to help, as well as deep faith as Catholics. Asking for volunteers needs to be supplemented by direct invitations to persons you feel are gifted for this type of religious education program.

Sometimes they may be persons who have never been involved in any parish program.

(4) Training. Provide a brief training workshop for all who will be involved in the VCS program. It is important that they all know one another and what each is expected to do. They all need to know the goals of the VCS, the curriculum materials and methodology to be used, and the desired atmosphere of fun-filled but serious religious education.

(5) Curriculum/textbooks. Some of the most successful parish VCS programs have been totally designed in the parish, including the curriculum, text materials, and related arts and crafts. Other parishes have successfully drawn on published Catholic or Protestant vacation programs. We are the authors of a successful two-year recyclable Catholic VCS program for one or two weeks: *Glad Days* and *Glory Days,* published by Silver Burdett Ginn.

We encourage you to explore further the possibilities of a VCS in your parish. Catholic vacation religious education programs have a long history and are used successfully by many Catholic parishes.

Part II

When? Where? How?

15.

How Adapt Your Textbook?

"We are using what many people say is an excellent textbook. I rather like it myself. But my fourth graders seem to get restless when we use it in class. I'm not sure what to do. I can't switch textbooks in midyear. What do you suggest?"

As authors of *This Is Our Faith* (Silver Burdett Ginn), we know how valuable a textbook can be for catechists and religion teachers. But, as you are experiencing, a good text does not guarantee successful classes.

What we do, even when using our own textbooks, is to *adapt* the book's lesson plans.

Since no two catechists, groups of youngsters, or situations are exactly the same, it is necessary to adapt the lessons to suit *your teaching style,* your *students' learning styles,* and the *teaching-learning situation.*

Here are some ways we have found helpful for adapting the textbook's lesson plans.

(1) Read the lesson plan early. As soon as possible after you finish teaching a lesson, sit down and read carefully the next lesson. This allows your imagination time to play with creative alternatives.

Read the student material, the whole plan, together with any background notes for the catechist that may accompany it.

(2) Find a focus. It is important that you clarify for yourself *what* is the central content of the lesson, and *why* it is important to the lives of your students. Most textbooks state the lesson's theme and objectives. You need to put these in your own words, answering for yourself, *What exactly do I hope will*

happen in the students because of this lesson, and why is it important to their lives?

You might write out your answer to be sure it is clear to you. Then dig into the steps of the lesson. Most textbook lesson plans follow a dynamic process of relating the youngsters' daily lives with the Church's faith tradition.

(3) Look at life. The lesson plans usually begin with some typical experience in the lives of youngsters of the age you are teaching. You need to be very clear about the *what, why* and *how* of the step or steps devoted to exploring that experience. *What* is the experience? *Why* is it worth exploring? *How* does it fit into this particular lesson? In adapting the plan, follow the textbook's lead. For example, find a more exciting photo in a magazine or newspaper to use with or instead of the photo in the textbook. Or find a song, film or video that explores the same experience. Or have the students draw, paint, make a collage or slide-show of the same experience in their own lives.

Instead of just reading the book's story, have the youngsters role-play it. Or find a similar real-life story in a newspaper or magazine and make a worksheet with questions about it. Or read to them a piece of children's literature dealing with the same experience.

The key is to engage the youngsters in exploring reflectively an important part of their lives.

(4) Look at Catholic tradition. Lesson plans usually present next a Bible story, liturgical symbol, doctrinal or moral teaching, or the example of a saint or other admirable Christian that relates to the life experience in the previous step(s). It is important that you clarify for yourself the *what* and *why* of this step, as well as *how* this aspect of Catholic tradition relates to that life experience.

Adapting is again a process of finding active, engaging alternatives to supplement what is in the book. For example, texts typically present an adapted Bible story accompanied by an illustration of the story. Try having the youngsters dramatize the story, draw it, write a news report or TV documentary of the story, or do a video of it. Or read the story from the Bible itself or use another version of the story. Or find a film, filmstrip, video or piece of sacred art of the story. Or try acting out liturgical rituals and saints' lives. The key is to help the youngsters get deeper into the meaning of their faith tradition.

(5) Link life and faith. Most lesson plans conclude by having the youngsters draw together the life experience and the aspect of faith in some kind of active response.

Once again be clear on the *what, why,* and *how* of this step.

Lesson plans here usually suggest some form of prayer, decision, and/or action that provides a response to God's Word heard in the life experience and in the related aspect of Catholic faith tradition.

You might ask the youngsters to write their own prayer in place of one in the textbook. Or substitute an activity you feel is more challenging to your students. Or have them create ads that sell the message of Jesus to people today. Or ask them to put to the music of a popular song new lyrics that express how their faith touches their lives. Or they could create a rap version. The key in this final step is to help the youngsters themselves link their lives and their faith.

These are just a few hints we have found helpful in adapting lessons in a good religion textbook. Don't try too much at once. Begin by adapting one activity in a lesson plan. We hope you find your students becoming more involved.

16.

How Plan Class Time?

"There seems to be so much material in each chapter of the text. How can I decide which is the most important to cover? How can I plan my time? Is it better to spend more than one session on a chapter and cover it well, or cover more material less thoroughly?"

Very practical questions! We hope our suggestions will be as practical as your questions. Let's start with your last question.

More or Less Depth?

Our criterion whether to probe less material more thoroughly, or to "cover" more material in less depth, is normally on the side of less coverage, but greater depth. This may mean spending more than one session on some chapters, and doubling up or omitting others.

It seems far better, for example, to spend more time exploring Abraham's faith in relation to the students' experiences, questions and doubts, than to "cover" Abraham, Isaac, Jacob, Joseph and Moses quite superficially.

However, there are at times reasons to give a superficial overview of facts to provide a context for probing an important topic. For example, even briefly relating Abraham to Isaac, Jacob, Joseph and Moses may help students better grasp Abraham's role and importance.

What is important is that what the children learn actually speaks on a deeper level to their present experiences, questions and struggles. Such catechesis can help them grow in faith.

The key to unlocking the catechetical process is the ability to probe *below the surface* of daily experience and Catholic tradition. Religious faith grows through *depth* experiences, not superficial data.

More or Less Important?

You ask about ways to decide which of the material in a textbook is most important to teach. We feel the answer to this question lies in a creative balance between four important factors:

(a) what the textbook suggests as more important in a given lesson. This is normally clear from the stated theme and aim of the lesson and the often unstated but discernible objectives of each of the lesson's steps. It is helpful to write out the lesson's theme, aim and objectives and mull over them in relation to these other factors:

(b) what you feel most strongly about regarding the theme, aim, and objectives of the lesson. Catechesis is a sharing of personal faith, not the mere passing on of what one reads in a textbook. So take some time to discern from inside yourself what you honestly feel is most important in the lesson. Jot it down.

(c) what your students experience, need, want and question in relation to what the textbook and you believe to be important. You can become surer of their readiness, questions and experiences by getting to know them better as the year goes on.

You can also give them simple "pre-tests" earlier to discover more of where they really are regarding the lesson's topic and objectives.

Write down what parts of the lesson you now feel would be most helpful to them here and now.

(d) what is happening of interest and importance outside of the class—in the parish, the school at large, your town or city, the broader Church and world. It may be that some parts of

your lesson take on fresh importance because of a current political event, liturgical feast or season, natural catastrophe, or cultural trend. Note what seems significant.

Then weigh the four factors and make your decision as to what in the lesson plan seems most important. Formulate in a few words what you most want your students to personally own from the lesson.

Select Activities

Then go through the lesson plan and select *one major activity* in *each step*. Trust your experience and judgment in making necessary choices among the text's activities.

In each step select the one major activity that you feel can best achieve your objectives.

Note also one or two other activities you would like to use if you should have time left.

More or Less Time?

Experience is the best guide to determining how much time to give to each part of the lesson. Here are three tips we suggest until you feel more comfortable.

1. Set arbitrary time limits. If you have 60 minutes for class, plan in terms of 45—to allow time for the unpredictable.

Then divide the 45 minutes into equal segments, one for each of the lesson's steps. You may adjust this as the class actually unfolds.

2. Time whatever has fixed limits. If you plan to use a piece of children's literature, a recorded song or instrumental music, or a film or video clip, actually time yourself reading the book aloud, listening to the song or music, or viewing the film or video clip.

3. Test the time of new activities. At first, time how long it takes you to do an activity you plan to have the students do, like drawing a Gospel story, making a mobile, writing a poem.

We find these hints helpful for planning our class time. We hope you do, too. As you grow in experience, you will discover your own unique ways to plan time better.

17.

How Discover Children's Experiences?

"The lessons in our textbook always start with the children's experience. Sometimes what is suggested doesn't seem to strike a chord with my students—like it doesn't reflect their experience. If integrating their experience with the focus of the lesson is so important, how can I discover what their experience is?"

Touching the real experience of those we catechize is, as you suggest, critical to effective catechesis. Here are some practical ways we have found helpful to discover the authentic life experiences of those we catechize.

Ask Them

The best source is obviously the children themselves. Make every effort to get to know them informally. Be available to chat with them before and after class.

In your religion classes you can enable them *directly* or *indirectly* to share their experiences in relation to the focus of a lesson. *Direct* asking will be effective only to the extent that you create a climate of mutual trust so the children feel comfortable sharing personal experiences. Here are some effective direct approaches:

(1) Questioning. Simply ask about their experience of what the textbook suggests, e.g., "When have you experienced how important it is to trust someone?" "Tell us a brief story of a time you helped someone in need." Be sure to listen sensitively to their words and their body language as they respond.

(2) Writing. Children tend to share more honestly and thoroughly through writing since there is more time for reflection and less social pressure from the group. "Write a poem about being afraid." "Write a story about the most difficult decision you have ever had to make."

(3) Drawing/Painting. We like to ask those we teach to draw an experience. "Draw a time you were hurting and someone helped you." "Draw how it feels to be lonely." The colors and lines add important feeling tones that reveal more at times than a spoken or written description of an experience. We normally ask the children to talk about their drawing or painting.

(4) Acting-out/Role-playing. Active, bodily ways of getting at the children's life experiences can be both enjoyable and revealing. Invite individuals or teams to act out a real or imagined experience. "Act out a time you were tempted to steal something." "Dramatize a time you did something you are really proud of." "Role-play yourself and your parents dealing with their need for you to clean your room."

Invite Them

Indirect approaches invite children to share their own experiences by responding to the experiences or creative work of others. This allows them to probe and talk about their own experience less self-consciously, and as a result, more honestly. Try these indirect approaches to their own experiences:

(1) Pictures. Show your students a strong photo or art work that pictures the experience called for by your lesson plan. Then invite them to talk about it, guiding them with questions like: "How does the picture make you feel?" "Why?" "What is/are the person/s doing, feeling?" "How well does the picture mesh with your own experience?"

(2) Music. Music is the privileged language of today's young people. We often play a popular song which touches an experience central to a lesson. Sometimes we duplicate the lyr-

ics for the students, inviting them to underline or circle words and phrases that speak most to their own experience. We then guide them in talking about the song and how well it reflects or illuminates their own experience.

(3) Stories/Poems. Good stories and poems hold up human experiences for leisurely appreciation and exploration. Children's literature is a rich mine of illuminating stories and poems. We often read in class a piece of children's literature that deals with a lesson's key experience. From the children's discussion of the story or poem, we—and they—learn much about their experiences.

Ask Others

In addition to these direct and indirect ways of enabling our students to share with us their true experiences, we can also gain insights from sources like these:

(1) Experts. Read an educational or developmental psychology book or journal about children the age and culture of those you teach.

(2) Parents. Get to know the parents of your students. They are often able to share insights into their youngster's experiences.

(3) Other Catechists. More experienced catechists can often help you better understand the experiences of those you catechize.

(4) Children's Literature. Few things can provide you with as much insight into children's experiences as the regular reading of children's literature—not primarily for use in class, but for your own enrichment.

With these and similar approaches we hope you will be successful in discovering and tapping into your students' real experiences as they relate to the themes of your textbook's lessons.

18.

How Foster Self-esteem?

"I've been noticing more and more articles in news-papers and magazines about the poor self-image of so many children and youth in our country. It got me wondering what I could do in my religion classes to build kids' self-esteem."

Over the past 10 years the increase in child suicides, the number of books on self-esteem, and our own observation, have led us to be more intentional about fostering the self-esteem of children in our once-a-week religion sessions.

The key is not found as much in special self-esteem building techniques as in genuine relationships with those we cate-chize. That means really caring about them, and investing something of ourselves in them and their growth.

Then certain skills or techniques can be helpful in fostering self-esteem and better self-images among those we teach. Here are some we have found helpful.

• *Prepare carefully for classes.* Coming to class well pre-pared says to the children, "I feel you are important. I really care about you." It also suggests to them that you think about them outside of class time, and that you feel they are worth your time and energies.

• *Know and use their names.* Few things are as important to self-esteem as being recognized by name. Knowing chil-dren's names is a primary sign of your care and esteem. Learn names early and use them often.

• *Remember important facts about the children's lives.* Try to remember the names of family members, friends, places and things—like pets, games, personal likes and dislikes, ages, birthdays, schools. Make a special effort to remember things individuals have said or done in your classes. When you recall in class something a child said, wrote, or did months earlier, you convey to a child a sense of his or her worth.

The famous longshoreman-become-philosopher, Eric Hoffer, writes of a woman who cared for him for several years when he was a child and blind: "Martha used to say again and again, 'You remember you said this, you remember you said that'. . . . She remembered everything I said, and all my life I've had the feeling that what I think and what I say are worth remembering. She gave me that."

• *Listen with your heart as well as your ears.* Eric Hoffer was fortunate to have someone who listened to him. In our busy society, few adults really listen to children. Work at developing your listening skills. Overcome your impulse immediately to give advice. Listen with your heart. Try to reflect back to the child what you have heard, especially on a feeling level. It is vital that children have opportunities to express their feelings. Do not be quick to judge.

• *Be available.* We have found that children are more open to talk about themselves in the moments before and after class. We try to arrive early and leave late so we have free time just to chat.

Just being there for them and with them tells them you care about them, and that affirms for them their own importance, since few things are as valuable as time.

• *Praise and affirm.* Children tend to blossom when they are appreciated, affirmed and honestly praised. Direct your praise to specific things a child says or does, so that the child knows you are really giving attention and learns from your praise specific abilities he or she may have.

• *Condemn actions, not individuals.* Be careful not to suggest to a child that he or she is a "bad," "lazy," "dishonest," "untrustworthy" person. Focus criticism on specific actions that may be negative. This allows a child to recognize unacceptable behavior and provides an opportunity for improvement without fostering a negative self-image.

• *Use "I" Messages.* Instead of saying, "You are making me angry!" try something like, "I am beginning to feel angry because there is so much talking."

The first blames a child or the group of children. It suggests they are somehow "bad." The "I" message of the second lets the children recognize their negative behavior and its impact on you, without putting them down.

• *Provide opportunities for children to share, to help, to contribute.* A major self-esteem-building experience for all children is to be able to make meaningful contributions to the teaching-learning experience. They can help with keeping order, taking roll, caring for and operating media equipment, as well as contributing ideas, feelings and even media, like contemporary rock songs that fit your lessons.

• *Share something of yourself with them.* Often we catechists teach our lessons and work hard to help the children learn about God, Jesus, the Church's teachings, but we may hesitate to let them learn anything about us as persons. We ask them to share their experiences, ideas and feelings, while we share little or nothing of our own lives with them. Mutual sharing reveals respect and trust, thereby fostering self-esteem.

To sum up, grow to love the children as individuals who matter to you, and sharpen some of the above esteem-building skills.

19.

How Be More Multicultural?

"Our neighborhood and parish have been changing rapidly. Now it's like a mini-UN with many Salvadorans, some Koreans, Vietnamese and Blacks, along with the white majority, mostly Polish, German, Irish and Italian. I'm wondering what to do as a catechist with children having so many different backgrounds?"

Your experience is common in an increasingly pluralistic, multicultural nation and Church. Your question is both timely and urgent.

Catechesis today needs to be consciously *multicultural*. That is, we must nurture in ourselves and our students knowledge and respect for our own and others' culture, race, and ethnic heritage. (see *National Catechetical Directory*, # 194).

Culture's Impact

Each of us grows up within a particular culture that colors every aspect of our lives, including how we hear God's Word and live out our Catholic faith. Recently our goddaughter, Angela Barbieri, watching Carl prepare a spaghetti dinner chided him, "You will never be Italian!" Carl laughingly responded, "And you'll never be German!"

Culture is so much a part of our lives that we tend to take it for granted. Fr. Virgilio Elizondo describes it as "that world in which we feel at home and among our own."

We tend to view *our* way of life as normative. Many ignore, avoid, look down on, or fear other cultures since they are different.

Multicultural catechesis aims at helping people appreciate the face of Christ in the faces of those of various cultures. Sr. Thea Bowman said God gave us five fingers to remind us that God's image is black, brown, white, yellow and red.

Our task as catechists in multicultural settings is to call forth the best from each group for the benefit of all.

Experts like Dr. Marina Herrera suggest five progressive stages in a truly multicultural catechesis: *awareness* (of cultural differences and similarities), *understanding* (of what is behind different cultural attitudes and practices), *acceptance and respect* (as human beings with equal rights), *appreciation and valuing* (as bearing gifts that can balance and benefit those of other cultures), and finally *selective adoption* (integrating those gifts into one's own culture and teaching).

Some Practical Tips

Such multicultural catechesis requires—even more than does any catechesis—a climate in your class that welcomes sharing, listening, and testing ways different people express their faith.

Within a warm, open atmosphere, try simple ways like these to make your catechesis more multicultural:

(1) Invite students to "show and tell" typical foods, games, clothing, art, music, especially religious objects and pictures, from their homes.

(2) Show pictures, films or videos portraying religious symbols and practices from around the world.

(3) Ask students to draw or write about favorite religious customs and family practices.

(4) Invite in parents or grandparents, or other representatives of various cultures, to talk about their culture and faith.

(5) Engage students in research into stories, traditions, proverbs, legends, songs, prayers and rituals, great women and men of their own and other cultures.

(6)   Set up "learning centers" with resources that provide insight into religious practices of various cultures. Encourage dialogue. Help older students to reflect critically on the strengths and weaknesses of their own and others' culture.

(7)   Display art of Jesus, Mary, saints, Bible stories and religious symbols created by artists of different cultures.

(8)   With your students, select religious art, symbols, stories, music, and rituals from diverse cultures for use in your classes. Weave stories, songs, symbols from the different cultures into your lessons and worship celebrations. Include some brief prayers and songs in the languages represented in your class.

(9)   Enrich Church seasons with cultural celebrations like *posadas* and *Kwanzaa.*

(10)   Mark the class calendar with feast days from around the world. Celebrate feasts of Mary, saints and other heroes and heroines from various lands.

(11)   Let snacks represent a variety of different foods typical of different cultures.

(12)   Occasionally wear an item of clothing that is African, Hispanic, Native American, or Asian.

(13)   You might find it most helpful personally to visit homes of your students of different cultures, and even to have classes or celebrations in different homes.

In these ways you can help your class embrace the attitude expressed by Dr. Herrera: "I want what is best of you (and your culture) to be part of what is best of me (and my culture)." Then all can experience the rich diversity of Christ's Church, which is becoming for the first time in history a truly global, multicultural, "catholic" Church, open to and embracing all.

20.

How Be an Environmental Catechist?

*"My two children are always reminding me to sepa-
rate recyclable materials from other trash. They
learn this at their schools. I'm beginning to wonder
if, as a catechist, I should be doing something along
environmental lines in my classes."*

Our two godchildren do the same for us. They let us know
exactly what and how to recycle. They, too, have become envi-
ronmentally aware through their schools.

Since schools, media and publishers do more and more to
foster environmental awareness and actions, we catechists can
use and affirm their contributions. For example, draw upon
magazines like *National Geographic* and its school version,
World, and books like *50 Simple Things Kids Can Do To Save
The Earth,* by The Earthworks Group.

Our special focus as catechists can then be to bring a
Catholic perspective to environmental and ecological issues.

Catholic Beliefs

Three aspects of Catholic belief seem particularly relevant:

(1) Creation. We believe God personally creates and
entrusts all creation to women and men—made in God's image—to enjoy, cultivate, care for, develop and share as God's
stewards. Earth, air, water, space, and all living things are good
and are God's gifts to all human beings. From the start, God,
people and the earth are intimately linked.

(2) Incarnation. As Christians we believe that God actually entered our space, took on our flesh, breathed our air, drank our water, walked our earth as Jesus of Nazareth. Jesus enjoyed the good things of creation, used them with respect and care, and warned against greed and selfishness in their use.

The New Testament suggests that the whole created world somehow shares in the saving presence and actions of the risen Christ. Paul praises Christ Jesus as the one in whom all creation holds together.

(3) Sacramentality. Believing that material things are created by God and graced by God's Incarnate Son, Catholics believe all created things can reveal and bring us into contact with God. For Catholics the normal way God approaches us and we respond is through people and things.

We can discover and meet God everywhere, in everyone and everything, because each person and thing is a sacrament of the living God. Every bush can be a "burning bush."

Catholic Spirituality

Reflecting these beliefs is the traditional Catholic use of ordinary things and natural symbols in the liturgy, popular devotions, and family rituals. Catholic life and worship exhibit a rich use of created things to express faith.

A genuinely traditional Catholic spirituality nurtures positive attitudes to created reality, material things, and natural resources. Among these faith-filled attitudes catechists can deepen in relation to environmental concerns are:

- *gratitude* to God for all of creation

- *appreciation* of created reality as the gift of God, bearing the love and presence of God, the gift-giver

- *wonder and awe* at the beauty and power of the universe as a reflection of God's awesome beauty

- *respect* and *reverence* for the earth, material things and natural resources as sacraments of God's loving presence

- *creativity* in exploring, using, developing and sharing the fruits of God's creative act

- *responsibility* and *care* in how we treat created reality, as God's stewards as well as consumers

- *justice* and *compassion* in the sharing of created reality for the good of all human beings.

Catechetical Helps

Here are some ways of sharing the above Catholic beliefs and spirituality as a catechist:

- *Bible.* Open your students to biblical passages that view the created world as gifts and signs of God's loving presence, e.g., Genesis 1-2, Job 38-39, Sirach 42-43, Psalms 8, 19, 104, Ephesians 1, Colossians 1.

- *Saints and other great Christians.* Share the example and words of great Christians who reveal a special appreciation for the created world, e.g., Francis of Assisi, Hildegard of Bingen, Meister Eckhart, Patrick, Thomas Aquinas, Ignatius Loyola, Catherine of Siena, Teresa of Avila, Thérèse of Lisieux, Teilhard de Chardin, Thomas Merton.

- *Sacramentals.* Make use in your classes of "sacramentals" like holy water, candles, statues, blessings, gestures like bowing, breathing deeply, processing, enthroning the Bible. Celebrate liturgical seasons with symbols like the Advent wreath, Christmas tree, ashes, palms.

- *Religious Imagination.* Stir your students' imaginations and feelings in relation to the wonders of creation through poetry, literature, art, music, science, and the electronic media. For example, read children's books like Douglas Wood's *Old Turtle,* Gloria Rand's *Prince William,* Miriam Schlein's *The Year of the Panda,* Deborah Lee Rose's *The People Who Hugged The Trees,* Thomas Locker's *The Land of the Gray Wolf,* and *Brother Eagle, Sister Sky—A Message from Chief Seattle.*

We hope these brief thoughts help you enrich your students' environmental awareness with a Catholic faith perspective.

21.

How Use Cooperative Learning?

"My daughter is in sixth grade. She does most of her homework on the phone with her friends, and says her teacher wants them to work together. Actually her grades are better this year. That got me wondering about having my religion students work together more. What do you think?"

We've had the very same experience and question. Our twelve-year-old goddaughter does much of her classwork and homework with her friends—and gets good grades.

Over the past several years, we have increasingly invited our students to work together in our religious education classes. The youngsters learn more, get along better, and seem to enjoy the classes more. Many of them are used to "cooperative learning" in their schools.

Cooperative Learning in Catechesis?

"Cooperative learning" is an important approach that has developed in general education over the past two decades. In cooperative learning students *work together in small groups to help each other learn.* Each individual *depends on* the members of the group and is *accountable to* them for learning. Mottoes: "I can succeed only if you do." "We all sink or swim together."

As catechists and religion teachers, one of our major tasks in the Church is to foster community, helping our students discover and share their unique gifts, thereby "building up the Body of Christ" (Ephesians 4:1-16). We and our students are each called at Baptism to minister to one another in a global, multicultural Church.

Cooperative learning, then, can fit in well with our catechetical goals.

How Do Cooperative Learning?

As a developed educational approach, "cooperative learning" normally requires special training. Without becoming experts in cooperative learning, catechists may draw upon its principles and methods.

Here are a few examples:

(1) Foster a sense of positive interdependence. Help the youngsters realize that they can each *benefit* from others' insights and can *contribute* their own unique gifts to everyone else in the group. "Two heads are better than one."

(2) Encourage a sense of individual responsibility. Help them grasp that each of them is responsible for his or her own learning as well as for helping other group members learn. Don't allow any individual to "get by" on the work of others or opt out of the group learning process.

(3) Form small, heterogeneous groups. Keep the groups to two or three members. Place together youngsters who differ in abilities, attitudes, as well as cultural and racial backgrounds. Differences are a key to successful cooperative learning teams, as well as to vitality and growth in the Church.

(4) Give them some learning tasks that can only be accomplished if all work together. For example, you might expect every individual in each group to be able to write out the eight Beatitudes. Group members need to help each other until each member knows all the Beatitudes.

(5) Give them learning tasks that do not have one "right" answer or solution. For example, ask each group to use magazine pictures and headlines to show what the first Beatitude might mean today. Open questions foster reflection, sharing, and creativity.

(6) Encourage learning of needed social skills as well as the learning of catechetical content. Such skills include contributing to the group, listening, trusting others, explaining one's ideas and feelings, respecting differences, and resolving conflict.

(7) Observe the youngsters as the groups work, noting down how well they work together, as well as how well they are learning the lesson's content.

Some Possibilities

These insights of cooperative learning experience may be introduced gradually into your teaching in a variety of ways, for example:

(1) Activities. Some activities—like dramatizing a Bible story, role-playing a common life-experience, making a video, and carrying out service projects—require students to work together.

Many other activities found in lesson plans may be done cooperatively as well or better than individually. For example, instead of having each child create one of the Stations of the Cross—as the lesson plan called for—we had pairs work together in creating each Station.

(2) Discussion. Encourage groups to discuss questions that textbooks expect individuals to answer.

(3) Memorization. Youngsters working together can help each other memorize definitions, dates, places, and other factual information.

(4) Research. Instead of each child learning all about a saint's life, have small groups explore segments and share their learnings with the whole class.

(5) Prayer. Try having students working in small groups develop simple prayer experiences.

(6) Testing. Youngsters in small groups can evaluate together what they have learned or missed.

You may find it helpful to cooperate with other catechists in exploring additional ways for your students to help each other learn about and grow in Catholic faith.

22.

How Get the Most Out of Catechetical Magazines?

"I like The Catechist's Connection and your columns. But when I actually sit down to plan a lesson, I often can't remember the details of something I read that would fit my lesson perfectly. And I'm not sure what year and what issue it was in, or where in the basement it might be. How can I remedy this?"

We've often felt the same frustration as we searched through four or five years' back issues, looking for a perfect activity we vaguely remember.

Our recommendation is to approach each issue of *The Catechist's Connection (Religion Teacher's Journal, Catechist,* or other educational journal) like a *meal.*

How *eat* a magazine? Try this:

Smell and Taste

When the magazine arrives, open it immediately. Glance through the issue the way you would look at a menu or foods at the next table, just to stimulate your appetite and whet your thirst. Then set it aside and go on with your work.

Nibble

From time to time, when you need a break, a mental "pick up," nibble at your magazine. Read a book review, brief article, ad or column. If you read something you'd like to cut out later, mark it clearly. Then leave the magazine handy so you can pick it up for another nibble later.

Bite and Chew

Save the longer articles for times when you have more peace and leisure. Sit back and read whatever article attracts you. There is no need to read a magazine from beginning to end. It's better to bite into whatever part seems most appetizing at the moment.

Read the article carefully, but quickly. That may be sufficient. If it seems to have real promise, excites and stimulates you, read it again, this time slowly, thoughtfully. Chew it. Digest it. Underline or hi-lite parts that seem particularly meaningful. Stop and mull over such sentences or segments. Bounce it against your own experience and insights.

A solid, provocative article is even worth outlining or mapping. You might want to copy out key words or phrases to make them your own. Not every article is worth such time and effort, but often in our haste we fail to mine the riches of thoughtful, practical articles.

Share a Bite or Two

Few of us like to eat alone. Eating with others makes food taste even better. So it is with catechetical reading. When you find an idea, activity or article that really turns you on, share it with other catechists. Clip it out, talk about it, critique it, develop it.

Set Some Aside for Snacks

Catechetical magazines often contain poems, prayers, inspirational stories, cartoons, quotations, photos, or carefully selected art works that you can come back to over and over for a snack. Cut them out. Put them on the refrigerator door, bulletin board, desk or table, dresser or bathroom mirror. It's a shame to enjoy these gems just once and then turn the page.

Freeze the Rest

When we find a bargain at the supermarket, we often cook some and freeze the rest. So it is with bargains like good catechetical newspapers and magazines. It is a good idea to "freeze" those parts of each issue that you find most helpful and think you might use later.

All you need is a "freezer"—an empty box, drawer, or a simple file system. Cut out the articles and other items you want to save. Toss them into your designated box or drawer. When you are preparing a lesson, you will at least know where to find that perfect idea, article, or activity you remember reading earlier.

If you are more systematic, set up a simple file system according to the themes of your textbook's lessons, or according to general topics like "Creative Ideas," "Bible," "Prayers," "Pictures," "Activities," etc. Arrange folders alphabetically and file what you want to save.

In this way you will be building your own home-resource center with all kinds of ideas, activities, stories, visuals, poems, quotations, prayers that you can turn to when you are preparing lessons during the year. Your "freezer" will be stocked with items you yourself found to your taste and liking—thereby making for much more personal, meaningful classes.

Order Dessert

Most issues of catechetical resources mention new materials, review new books, or introduce you to interesting people. Take some time with what is left of your respectfully carved up magazine to write for helpful items you or your parish might use. Write for more information, order a book, video or other resource, or invite a speaker.

These will come later to top off your meal like a good dessert.

So instead of just perusing such valuable monthly materials, "eat" them—smell and taste, nibble, bite and chew, share, snack, freeze, and order dessert. You'll find yourself greatly enriched.

And, if you later need or want to see a particular issue as a whole, your parish or school library no doubt will have a complete set for reference.

23.

How Find Meaning of Bible Stories?

"I have always enjoyed teaching the stories of Jesus' birth at Christmas time. But now I'm upset and puzzled. Our pastor told us that there was no star, no Wise Men, maybe not even a stable. If that's true, then how am I to make sense out of these stories and teach them?"

In the past 150 years or more, scholars have carefully studied the Bible using modern scientific techniques. For example, they analyze the "infancy narratives" about Jesus' birth (Matthew 1-2; Luke 1-2) to see who wrote them, when, where, why and for whom they were written.

This approach to the Bible, called *historical criticism*, has immeasurably enriched our understanding of the Bible, while also causing the kind of concern you feel about the star, Magi and manger.

Historical criticism discovered, for example, that the infancy narratives in Matthew and Luke are not historical accounts, much less documentaries, but stories carefully crafted to announce the main themes of the good news according to Matthew and Luke. These stories are full of allusions to Old Testament stories, prayers and prophecies.

Literary Criticism

We may understand these beloved Christmas stories, then, the same way we try to understand any good story. A more recent approach to understanding the Bible, called *literary criticism*, deals with Bible stories precisely as stories.

So dig into the Gospel stories of the Christmas season with anticipation. The star, Magi, and manger are still part of the stories, and their meaning is found in their role in the stories as you read them.

How to Read a Bible Story

Here are some suggestions based on the *literary* approach:

(1) Read the text carefully. No matter how well you think you know the stories of Jesus' birth, it is critical that you read the actual text of Matthew 1-2 and Luke 1-2 carefully, one at a time. Read with a pencil or hi-liting pen in hand. Note any details that strike you—words, expressions, images—and any thoughts, feelings or questions that surface in you.

(2) Analyze the story. Then study the Gospel story the way you might study any other story. That means, in language you may remember from English class, looking at *plot, characters, setting* and *literary techniques.* Simply put, pay close attention to *who* does *what, when, where, why* and *how* in the story, and *how* the story writer put the story together to create a meaningful, interesting narrative.

Using Literary Analysis

• *What happens,* and *how?* ("plot"). Stories usually begin with a situation of tension, conflict or ambiguity. Each event then tends to raise more questions, give clues, increase the ambiguity and tension, building to a climax and resolution.

So, divide up a long Gospel story into "acts" or "scenes," by noticing changes in time or place, the arrival or exit of characters, shifts from description to dialogue. Look for similarities and contrasts between the acts or scenes. Do this first with Matthew 1-2, then with Luke 1-2, then compare the two. For example, notice what events are in only one Gospel, or in both.

• *Who does what,* and *why?* ("character"). A story's plot normally hinges on the actions and words of people in the story. Some characters are more important, more developed, than others, especially the *main character,* the one whose actions most influence the plot.

We learn about characters and their motivation by what they do, and by what they say to or about themselves. Look carefully at the various characters, their words, actions and relationships.

Notice, for example, who comes to visit the newborn king and who does not. Compare the roles of Mary and Joseph in the two Gospels.

• *When* and *Where?* ("setting"). The places and times in which the plot develops can also reveal something of a story's meaning. Setting can create a mood, give insight into a character, heighten tension, arouse curiousity, shock or soothe.

Notice for example where Jesus is born, the star, the fact that he is born during the night. What do these say about him and his mission?

• *Literary techniques.* Biblical authors, like all storytellers, use devices to involve us in their story and to convey meaning. Some such techniques are surprise, similarity and contrast, questions, repetition of key words and images, irony, and parallelism. Notice for example the similarities and differences between the stories of Jesus' birth and John the Baptist's birth in Luke. Compare Matthew's and Luke's techniques.

(3) Contextualize it. Make use of references given in most Bibles to look up the Old and New Testament texts used by Luke and Matthew. This can help you see these stories in relation to the Old Testament and to the rest of Matthew and Luke.

(4) Pray it. Invite the Holy Spirit to help you relate the story to your own life and contemporary society, and help you respond to God's Word to you.

Try this approach. It may provide a fascinating new look at these stories. You can readily adapt this approach to your students' ages and abilities.

24.

How Teach About Mary?

"It's almost May, and I'm wondering what to do. May used to be Mary's month and we always had a May crowning. Is that still done? I have the feeling that we now play down Mary. Should we still teach the Rosary? I don't know what to do about Mary any more."

Your confusion is not unusual. There has been a rather dramatic change in the Church's approach to Mary over the past quarter-century.

Many of us share your memories of a time when Marian devotions, feasts, shrines, prayers, hymns, and practices dominated Catholic spirituality. So much so that Protestants accused us of "mariolatry."

From Goddess to Sister

Catholic "mariology" and Marian devotions then stressed Mary's exalted status and queenly privileges. Mary was viewed almost as a goddess, looking down lovingly from on high on us sinful humans.

Without downplaying Mary's unique role as Mother of God, Vatican Council II in the early 1960s stressed less her exalted titles and privileges than her close ties to humanity, to the Church, and to Jesus. (See Chapter 8 of the Council's document, *The Church*.)

Following the Council's lead, scholars and pastors worked to reshape Marian theology and devotions.

Blending Old and New

The result has been an approach to Mary that respects Catholic doctrines about Mary—her motherhood of God, virginity, immaculate conception and assumption—but reinterprets them in accord with the biblical, liturgical, ecumenical and social sciences.

"Older" images and titles of Mary—Mother of God, God-bearer, Queen of Heaven, Our Lady—are balanced with "new" images and titles of Mary like the following:

• *Our sister.* Mary is in solidarity with all human beings, sharing our humanness, looking with us to God and her Son for salvation.

• *Woman of faith.* This title reflects the core inner attitude of Mary as described in the Gospels—her faith, that is, her total trust in God and surrender to God's will.

• *Model disciple of Jesus.* The New Testament portrays Mary as the first and best disciple of Jesus. As such she is the model of Christian discipleship, of what followers of Jesus are to be like.

• *Model of the Church.* The New Testament places Mary within the community of Jesus' disciples and suggestively identifies Mary with the Church. Mary is not only Mother of the Church, but Model of what the Church is to become.

• *Prophetess of justice.* Mary's hymn, the Magnificat (Lk 1:46-55), praises God who rights injustice, puts down the mighty who oppress the poor, raises up the weak and fills those who hunger.

• *Liberated and liberating woman.* Placing her trust in God and in her Son, Jesus, Mary first experiences full liberation from sin's power and works with God to free her brothers and sisters from the powers of evil.

Practical Guidelines and Tips

Our challenge as catechists is to be like the head of a household "who brings from his storeroom both the new and the old" (Matthew 13:52).

To help us in this task, we have four guidelines which Pope Paul VI set out in 1974 in his encyclical, *Marian Devotions.* According to the Pope, Marian theology and devotions need to be:

- *biblical,* respecting the Scriptures as a primary source;

- *liturgical,* in harmony with the Church's liturgy;

- *ecumenical,* sensitive to the faith of other Christians; and,

- *anthropological,* responding to the social and cultural needs and knowledge of our time.

Following these guidelines, we catechists can creatively lead our students to a knowledge and love of Mary that may both comfort and challenge them. For example:

- *Use the Bible* as a primary source, especially Matthew 1-2; Luke 1-2; 4:16-30; 8:19-21; 11:27-28; John 2:1-12; 19:25-29; Acts 1:12-2:4; Revelation 12:1-6.

- *Celebrate* Marian feasts, drawing upon the readings, prayers, and hymns found in the *Lectionary* and *Sacramentary.*

- *Make the most of traditional Marian times,* like May and October, as rich opportunities to learn more about Mary and to pray to her.

- *Enrich traditional practices,* like May processions and crownings, with readings, images, prayers and hymns that reflect the direction of Vatican II and recent Marian theology.

- *Teach and pray the Rosary* which draws so fully from the Bible and focuses so strongly on Jesus.

- *Study and occasionally use traditional prayers and hymns* like the Hail Mary (*Ave Maria*), Litany of Loreto, Angelus, Hail Holy Queen (*Salve Regina*), *Memorare*, and Queen of Heaven (*Regina Coeli*).

• *Learn and use new prayers and hymns* like the Pax Christi *Litany of Mary of Nazareth*, or prayers and hymns from the Third World. Or have your students write their own hymns and prayers to Mary.

• *Expose students to good art* of Mary, drawing upon sacred art of many ages and cultures to reveal what Mary means to diverse peoples.

We hope this has been of some help to you. For a further insights into Mary, try Anthony Tambasco's excellent book, *What Are They Saying About Mary?* (Paulist Press, 1984).

25.

How Teach Church History?

"I've had it with history. Kids just don't take to it. I taught 6th grade last year—Old Testament. They were bored. Now I'm teaching 8th grade, and it's mostly Church history. They're positively resisting me. What can I do besides quit?"

That's a tough question, one we hear over and over. We'd like to share with you some things we have found helpful in teaching historical parts of the Bible and Church history.

Four Basic Principles

1. Try to understand and love the youngsters. Your students have as yet little sense of history. They have only lived about a dozen years and are just developing a readiness for grasping large spans of time.

At their age they are caught up in tumultuous changes they experience in most parts of their lives. They are also growing up in a culture that shows little awareness or appreciation of the past.

What they need most from us catechists at this point are understanding and love. That may not change their boredom and resistance, but it will help you and your students be more patient and creative.

2. Relate past to present. Preteens and young teenagers by and large find historical data interesting or meaningful only when the past speaks to today's world. Good textbooks have this linkage of past and present built into lesson plans. But it is our challenge as teachers to creatively engage our students in making that link between past and present—and future—come alive.

For example, Francis of Assisi can become very relevant in grappling with today's issues of war, peace and the environment. The Hebrew prophets spoke a message of compassion and justice that our young growing up in a consumerist culture need to hear. The story of Judith speaks to feminist aspirations.

3. Keep it personal. Preteens and early teens are engulfed in confusing surges of growth in their whole being. They need to see historical events from a personal perspective that throws some light on their inner experiences. That means mostly through people.

The Bible and the Church's history are filled with fascinating people whose struggles, fears, desires, needs, temptations, successes and failures are not unlike those youngsters grapple with today.

David's lust, Jeremiah's insecurity, Ruth's friendship, Moses' yearning for freedom—and anxiety once he tasted it—Miriam's daring—all can touch a chord in young people's experiences today.

Stories of long-ago Christians, too,—like Frances of Rome, Genevieve of Paris, Thomas More, Dominic Savio—can help today's young reflect on and probe their own experiences.

4. Better more than much. Historical teaching often remains superficial by trying to cover too much. It is better at this age to get more deeply into a few key personalities and events than to touch on everything in more than 5,000 years of Judeo-Christian history. Better to explore the inner dynamic of what happened, why people did what they did, how they felt, and what the consequences of their actions were, than to skim the surface of countless names and dates.

Five Creative Techniques.

Keeping those principles in mind, here are a few helpful techniques to flesh them out.

1. Invite in guest speakers. For example, in teaching a lesson on monasticism, invite in a monk. Let him tell about his way of living and then answer questions. A rabbi or other faithful Jew might shed new light on a story from the Hebrew Scriptures, our Old Testament.

2. Use the news media. Magazines, newspapers, TV and radio can help make historical events come alive. Coverage of current events provides great photos and stories of peoples and lands closely related to biblical and historical events. The cities, peoples and struggles of those centuries-old stories are a staple of today's daily news.

3. Dramatize the stories. Invite your students to enter into historical stories by acting out some of them. In this way they can identify with personalities, feel their inner desires and struggles, grapple with their decisions. Youngsters this age tend to be active and to enjoy dramatizing if it is done sensitively. Do not hesitate to have them create costumes and props occasionally. Photographing the dramatization allows the students to create their own slide-sound show or video of the biblical or historical story.

4. Use music, poetry, art, prayers. Be as creative as possible in using various art forms. We use rock music in many classes with students of this age, because it is the atmosphere in which they live. Carefully selected poetry can be powerful, and personal. So, too, can art—sacred and secular, and strong photography, video and film.

Drawing, too, is useful. Meaningful prayer can pull everything together in the students' hearts and minds.

5. Take field trips. Take an occasional field trip to a local place of interest related to what your students are studying—like a museum, gallery, synagogue, mosque, tourist agency, monument, cemetery.

These are a few tips we have found helpful. We encourage you to try them before you give up.

26.

How Understand Junior High Kids?

"I'm teaching Junior High for the first time this year. So far it's been hard. I like the kids but I don't feel I understand where they are coming from. I'm not at all sure what they're really thinking and feeling. How can I get to know them and their world better?"

We've been teaching Junior High for the last few years and know well what you are wondering about.

Here are a few approaches we have found helpful in getting inside youngsters of this challenging age.

Getting to Know Them

(1) Be available and approachable. Young teenagers need to feel that you like them, enjoy being with them, and take them seriously. Just being there for and with them a few minutes before and after class gives them a chance to establish more personal ties with you.

Unless they sense your honest interest and care, they will hesitate to share with you their real concerns, questions, or interests.

(2) Give them opportunities to understand and express themselves. Young adolescents are going through a puzzling time of major changes in almost every area of their lives—body, feelings, friendships, expectations, responsibilities, schools, often families, too. They find it hard to express what they think and feel because they are not sure themselves. They are often self-conscious and halting in expressing themselves verbally. So, help them by giving them chances for *reflection* and *creative*

expression. You—and they—will be able to learn much about their world of experience through their own creative work.

(3) Let them work together often. Junior High youngsters tend to like doing things together. Any of the following activities may be done cooperatively as well as individually.

In an atmosphere of mutual care and understanding, let them explore and express who they are through creative activities, like the following:

(a) Invite them to *write* about experiences, issues, feelings, ideals, beliefs, and people. Encourage the writing of *journals* and *diaries, poems* and *original stories, worksheets* (e.g., based on a newspaper story, article, picture or cartoon), *letters,* or *essays.*

(b) Encourage them to *draw, paint, doodle, take photos* or *make videos,* so they can explore their lives and express without words what they cannot say verbally.

(c) Have them *act out, dramatize* and *make things,* thereby channeling their need for physical activity into reflection and expression.

(d) Give them time to evoke and name their inner world through the *visual arts*—like *painting, sculpture, photography, film,* and *video.*

(e) Let them enjoy and interpret *music,* especially *rock music,* as a unique way for you and them to look more deeply into their world.

Read About Them

(3) *Read professional books and journals.* Four *books* we have found invaluable are: David Elkind, *All Grown Up & No Place to Go* (Addison Wesley, 1984); Wayne Rice, *Junior High Ministry* (Zondervan, 1987); and Lynda Madaras, *The What's Happening to My Body Book for Girls,* and *The What's Happening to My Body Book for Boys* (both: New Market Press, 1988). Helpful *journals* include:

Religion Teacher's Journal (Twenty-Third Publications) and *Catechist* (Peter Li Publications)—both of which each month have at least one article on Junior High catechesis; *Group's Junior High Ministry,* and *Parents & Teenagers* (both: Box 407, Mt. Morris, IL 61054)—devoted just to understanding and working with teenagers; and Don Kimball's *Top Music Countdown* (Cornerstone Media, P.O. Box 6236, Santa Rosa, CA 95406)—a priceless resource for using rock music in ministry.

(4) Read children's literature. Perhaps an even more helpful resource for entering into the minds, hearts, and experiences of young adolescents is the fascinating world of books written specifically for them. Excerpts from such books can also be used in your classes.

Here are a few we have found very helpful for understanding our junior high students:

(inner feelings & questions) Bruce Brooks, *What Hearts?* (Harper Collins, 1992); Judy Blume, *What Kids Wish They Could Tell You—Letters to Judy* (Pocket Books, 1986); Jean Little, *Hey World, Here I Am!* (Harper & Row, 1986)—a book of poems and short essays; Cynthia Rylant, *Missing May* (Orchard Books, 1992); Walter Dean Myers, *Somewhere In the Darkness* (Scholastic, 1992), and by Gary Paulsen: *Hatchet* (Bradbury Press, 1987), *Popcorn Days and Buttermilk Nights* (E.P. Dutton, 1983), *The Island* (Dell, 1988), and *The River* (Delacorte Press, 1991).

(moral choices) Marion Dane Bauer, *On My Honor* (G.K. Hall, 1989); Gillian Cross, *On the Edge* (Holiday House, 1984); Eve Bunting, *Such Nice Kids*, (Houghton Mifflin, 1990); Margaret I. Rostkowski, *After the Dancing Days* (Harper & Row, 1986); Cynthia Voight, *Izzy, Willy-Nilly* (Ballentine, 1986).

(changing and maturing) Niels H. Lauersen and Eileen Stukane, *You're In Charge—A Teenage Girl's Guide to*

Sex and Her Body (Fawcett Columbine, 1993); Judy Blume, *Are You There, God? It's Me, Margaret* (Dell, 1970); and, Judy Blume, *Then Again Maybe I Won't* (Dell, 1971); Budge Wilson, *The Leaving* (Philomel Books, 1990); James Ramsey Ullman, *Banner in the Sky* (Harper & Row, 1988).

(divorce & separation) Elfie Donnelly, *Tina Into Two Won't Go* (Four Winds Press, 1983).

(curiosity and doubt about faith) Robert Cormier, *Other Bells For Us To Ring* (Delacorte Press, 1990).

Teaching Junior High is a challenge, but it can be most rewarding to you and richly beneficial to those you teach. We hope you find some of our tips helpful.

27.

How Plan Class Masses?

---

*"Can you share some tips for planning class liturgies?
Do we have to use the lectionary readings, or can a
special theme prevail? How can I get my students involved in planning and participating in a class Mass?"*

We always try to involve our students in a class Eucharist
each year. It often turns out to be the high point of the year for
both children and parents alike.

Our special Eucharistic liturgy is for our students and their
extended families. We usually celebrate it in the classroom or
home where our class normally meets, or in the parish church or
a chapel.

Invaluable for planning these celebrations is the Vatican's
sensitive *Directory for Masses with Children* (1974). What fol-
lows is in accord with that great document which so deeply respects children.

Enjoyable Participation

We aim at active participation, especially of the children. We
adapt many aspects of the Eucharistic celebration to allow for
greater understanding, delight, and involvement by the children.

In addition to participating in communal songs, prayers,
and gestures—like at their regular Sunday Eucharist—individual
children or teams may prepare the place and the altar, act as
cantor, play musical instruments, proclaim the readings, dramatize a reading, respond during the homily, recite general intercessions, bring gifts to the altar, and pray spontaneously.

Planning and Preparation

Careful planning by the children and yourself (perhaps with several parents) is critical. Here are key areas:

• *Central focus.* Instead of a rigidly-observed theme, look for some central focus to provide unity to the celebration. Using the new *Lectionary for Children*, look for this focus in the biblical readings for the day as they relate to something important to your group, what they have been learning, the feast or season, or some other significant experience or event. The central focus may be a symbol or metaphor rather than a clear conceptual idea. Imagination here is more important than logic, poetry more than prose.

• *Readings.* You may not omit the Gospel, but you may omit other biblical readings, or replace them with other readings from the Bible, or with an appropriate reading from another book, like a piece of children's literature—always in terms of your central focus. Involve the children in selecting the readings.

• *Music.* Determine together what songs, music and musical instruments you wish to use. Hymns or other appropriate songs related to your central focus may be used. Carefully selected recordings can also be very effective at times.

• *Prayers.* While the acclamations and responses to the greetings and invitations of the priest (e.g., Gloria, Creed—may use the Apostle's Creed—Sanctus, Memorial Acclamation, Great Amen, Agnus Dei), as well as the Lord's Prayer, are not to be omitted or adapted, they may be recited or sung to various melodies. The General Intercessions are to relate to genuine concerns of your children, their families, and to timely broader issues. These need to be written. You may also plan for other appropriate prayers, including spontaneous prayers.

Select together the prayers you wish to include, and any melodies or gestures to accompany them. You may choose one of the *Eucharistic Prayers for Children's Masses.*

• *Gestures and actions.* Children tend to be active and to learn through their whole bodies. Processions (e.g., at entrance, with the book, with the gifts, communion, and at end), gestures during prayers, songs or silence, and dramatizations can be very effective.

• *Visuals.* Visual images are very important. One or more banners, symbols, photos, drawings or sacred art works can provide a visualization of your central focus. The visual(s) may be prominently placed, or may be included in ritual actions (e.g., kissing a cross). We have had children prepare visuals at home with their families, who together carry them in a procession at Mass.

• *Environment.* Select a comfortable, flexible environment and prepare it as beautifully as possible. Carefully consider room arrangement for ease of seeing, hearing, and moving about.

• *Roles.* Select together which children will fill the various roles suggested above.

Obviously a key person will be the *Priest,* who ideally should be comfortable with children and able to communicate with them. The priest may adapt the prayers from the Roman Missal to make them more meaningful to children, and may insert brief, simple introductions and explanations as the Eucharist progresses. If the priest feels uncomfortable or unskilled speaking to children, you and he may invite another adult to speak to the children after the Gospel reading.

Parents and other adults should participate as fully as possible. We usually have the children sit with their families, except when occupied in actions involving just the children.

Class Eucharists can be graced, memorable moments when carefully, creatively prepared.

28.

How Do Class Prayer Services?

"Can you share some tips on class prayer services and prayer rituals? Do they always have to be based on the particular liturgical reading for the day, or can a special theme prevail? How go about planning them?"

From early times Christians have developed prayer services, prayer rituals, and popular devotions alongside the Church's official liturgy. These have had and continue to have an important place in catechesis.

The Second Vatican Council (1962-1965) recognized the validity of such devotions and prayer services, indicating that they should "harmonize with the liturgical seasons, accord with the sacred liturgy, [be] in some fashion derived from it, and lead people to it . . . ." (*Liturgy*, 13).

With those guidelines in mind, we catechists may freely create prayer rituals in our classes. They need not follow exactly the structure of the Liturgy of the Word, nor be limited just to symbols and prayers taken from the Liturgy of the Eucharist, other sacramental rites, or the Liturgy of the Hours.

Building Blocks

We may create prayer rituals for our classes by creatively using key elements of the Church's liturgy as "building blocks":

• *Reading*—normally from the Bible, but other sources that explore some aspect of the mystery of human experience are also valuable, e.g., a piece of children's literature, a letter, poem or story, an excerpt from a biography or novel.

- *Silence*—preparing for or following any of the other building blocks.

- *Music and/or song*—sacred or secular, traditional or modern, instrumental or vocal.

- *Prayer*—traditional or spontaneous, Christian or non-Christian, quiet or aloud, individual or group.

- *Images and/or symbols*—like photos, sacred and secular art, videos or films, natural and religious symbols (e.g., water, light/darkness, a flower, a rock, food).

- *Symbolic actions*—like blessing, anointing, signing, eating/drinking, dancing, giving/receiving, sign of peace, or new, creative actions.

We may freely arrange the building blocks in order best to fit our situation, and to foster a desired response.

These six traditional building blocks of Christian worship can engage the whole person and the community in the dynamic of listening to and responding to God's Word—by touching the heart, informing the mind, stirring the imagination and motivating to action.

Some Practical Tips

Here are some hints for creating effective prayer services.

1. Contextualize. Prayer services or rituals in catechetical settings normally need to flow from and be clearly related to a given lesson, liturgical feast or season, or some significant experience—like a birthday, class achievement, baptism, wedding, contemporary issue, or current event. In this way you and your students know the occasion and purpose for the prayer service.

2. Focus. There is no need to use the liturgical readings of the day, nor is there a need to have a clearly definable "theme." Sometimes attempting to center every element too narrowly on a predetermined conceptual theme can hinder spontaneous responses and stifle prayer.

Yet prayer services are normally more effective when they have a clearly-perceived unity—of feeling, ideas and images. Such unity comes from maintaining an uncluttered focus as you assemble the building blocks.

Test each building block in its relation to the others—does it fit? does it relate to and complement what went before and what comes after? does the whole move rhythmically through a beginning, middle and end?

3. Simplify. Simplicity is the key to effective prayer services. Avoid multiplying or duplicating ideas, images, symbols, actions.

At first select a biblical *reading,* a religious *song,* and a *prayer,* in that sequence—to exemplify the basic dynamic of hearing God's Word and responding to it.

Next, perhaps, try some carefully-selected *instrumental music,* or a *song* or *hymn,* to prepare for the reading. Or use a strong *visual symbol or image* to focus the imagination throughout. Or conclude the service with a *symbolic action.*

After you feel more secure, you may select quite different arrangements of these same building blocks, even using more than one at the same time—e.g., playing appropriate music quietly during a Bible reading or ritual action, uniting a hymn or song with a symbolic action. You may also drop one or more of the building blocks. But always keep the whole ritual contextualized, focused, and simple, around the basic dynamic of listening to and responding to God's Word.

4. Abbreviate. Normally keep prayer services or rituals shorter rather than longer, until you and your students feel a need or desire to extend them. Better to leave them with a taste and desire for more than tire or bore them.

We wish you well as you become more confident in this important element of catechesis.

29.

How Use Newspapers and Magazines?

"The youngsters in my religious education classes don't always take the stories and pictures in our textbook seriously. They say they aren't real. I like the textbook, but I know that at times I have to do something more. What about using newspapers and magazines?"

We find that our students sometimes have similar reactions. So we supplement the textbook with newspapers and magazines, as your question suggests. Sometimes we use what we find in place of, sometimes with, what is in the textbook.

Plan Ahead

To use magazines and newspapers creatively in a lesson requires planning. We use the textbook as our guide. It provides a plan, a "recipe," that we can enrich with resources like the *news media*.

We often prepare simple *work-sheets* to allow the youngsters to grapple with and respond to an item from the news media and relate it to the theme of a textbook lesson. For example, we clip a *photo* or *story* and place *questions* beside it—questions often from the lesson.

The key to using the news media effectively in lesson plans is to plan ahead. Become familiar with the textbook lessons at least a month or more ahead of time.

That look ahead alerts you to notice items in the newspapers and magazines you normally read that may be useful in upcoming lessons. You will be surprised how many things in the news relate to your classes.

Practical Tips

Here are some of the ways we use magazines and newspapers to enrich the lessons in our textbook.

(1) Pictures. We look carefully at the visuals in upcoming lessons, and then keep an eye out for photos, illustrations and art in the news media that convey similar images and messages. The news media are filled with real-life pictures of the very experiences pictured in textbooks.

We even find superb reproductions of good art, including religious art, in newspapers and magazines, particularly at certain seasons of the year.

(2) Comics. It is surprising how often the comic page meshes with life experiences, issues, or values found in our textbook lesson plans. Comics not only reflect human experience but their humor adds to their attraction and impact.

The same is often true of cartoons on the editorial page of papers and magazines. They cut to the heart of controversial issues, and add a sense of timeliness and urgency to what is prepared for textbook lessons.

(3) Ads. Advertisements for products as well as ads for jobs or personal relationships provide a rich resource for exploring many of the values and attitudes treated in catechetical textbooks. A well chosen ad can stimulate reflection and discussion in a way that a textbook question or illustration on the same topic often may not.

(4) Stories. Most religion textbooks are filled with stories, mostly written precisely for the lessons. Real-life stories on the very same topics abound in magazines and newspapers—on the news pages, in literary supplements, political analysis, and the editorial page.

Because the stories are taken from the news media they tend to have more interest and impact for students, while perfectly fitting the lesson plan.

(5) Editorials. The editorial page, too, can provide excellent material for probing real life issues and values. Editorials make fine discussion starters on the very themes of a textbook's lessons. Letters-to-the-Editor give opposing views of experiences and issues.

(6) News. News reports today take us to all parts of the world, often to the very places being studied in religion class. For example, the Gulf War took place in what centuries earlier was the world of Abraham. So much of the news about the Middle East is about the land and people Moses, David, Jeremiah and Jesus knew and loved.

Often news reports bring us examples of people who exemplify the ideals and virtues proposed in textbook lessons. These real-life, contemporary people may move youngsters more than the stories of dead saints in textbooks—or make the saints' lives more believable.

(7) Maps, charts, statistics. The news media regularly provide helpful graphic presentations of a wide variety of information related to the lessons in our textbook. This information is typically up-to-date and imaginatively presented.

(8) Prayers. Sometimes newspapers and magazines print powerful prayers of individuals in demanding situations, or struggling for rights or ideals. These add realism to textbook prayers.

Every day every newspaper or magazine as a whole provides material for a vast litany of prayers—for suffering people, for the success of vital causes, for needs of all kinds, prayers of thanks, of sorrow, of praise, of petition, of faith, hope and love. Youngsters can also write prayers that persons in news stories or pictures might pray.

These are just some of the ways newspapers and magazines can infuse "reality" into your textbook lessons. Good luck!

30.

How Use Videos?

"We just recently got several TV's and VCR's in our parish center. They are movable and we can use them for our religious education classes. I find that exciting, but I'm not sure how to use videos or TV in my classes. Can you help me?"

Since we teach in different parishes with varying facilities, we bought a small, easily portable, combination TV and VCR several years ago to use in our classes. We've found the impact of TV and videos on young and old is often considerably greater than earlier use of films and filmstrips.

Here are some tips drawn from our experience and reading.

Before

Before you use a video in one of your catechetical sessions, prepare carefully.

(1) Resources. Become aware of the various kinds of videos that may be useful in catechesis.

Most readily available are *popular* commercial videos found in video stores, supermarkets, and other stores—movies, documentaries, and music videos. They deal mostly with ordinary life experiences, contemporary issues or enduring questions, in compelling, often entertaining ways. Many have great potential for catechesis.

Less readily available are explicitly *religious* videos available from Catholic and other Christian publishers. These are often created specifically for use in religious education settings. Ask your parish or diocesan religious education director or parochial school principal or librarian for suggestions.

Then there are *homemade* videos, put together using widely available camcorders. You, your students, neighbors, family and friends are potential sources. Making a video together with your students can be a great experience.

(2) Purpose. Determine just why and how you want to use a video in your catechesis. To probe an experience or issue? To explore a Bible story, liturgical ritual, Church doctrine, saint's life? To relate some aspect of Catholic faith with contemporary life?

Do you want to use it mainly to encourage thinking? to raise questions? or to spark sharing and cooperative learning? or to nurture personal or group prayer? or to lead to some action or project?

Ask yourself exactly where and how it will fit in your lesson plan. A video is catechetically worthwhile only if it truly enhances and deepens the goals and meaning of your lesson.

(3) Preview. Never use a video without first previewing it carefully to be sure it fits into your catechetical goals.

Another reason to preview the video is to determine if and where you might want to pause during it, or which brief segment or scene you might use without showing the whole video. Sometimes a brief clip from a longer video can be more effective for your purposes in a class.

As you preview the video, be sensitive to key images, sounds, feelings, words, and turning points.

(4) Prepare helps. Once you have viewed the video, you may want to prepare a worksheet, for example, to guide the youngsters' response to the video. Or prepare questions to focus the students' viewing. See our suggestions further on.

(5) Test. Be sure to test the video in the TV/VCR equipment you will be using in your class, especially if you are not familiar with it—so you are sure how to turn it on, control picture and volume, pause, etc. Be sure also to check out the room arrangement so that all can easily see and hear the video.

(6) Prepare students. It is normally helpful to dig into the students' experience, knowledge and feelings about the topic the video will explore. This can foster interest, attention and curiosity.

Sometimes you can give them one or more questions to keep in mind as they watch the video. However, sometimes it is more effective to jump right into watching a video.

During

As you actually show the video, you and your students may simply view it quietly. Or ask them to take notes, jot down questions or reactions, or doodle creatively during it. Or pause the video at times to have the youngsters react to a segment by writing, drawing, discussing, or other creative activity. Then start the video for another segment. Or freeze a particular frame and engage the students with it—e.g., writing what a character might feel, want, or pray for, or do. Or stop the video before it ends and ask the youngsters to suggest their own endings.

After

After the video, follow up on it according to your lesson plan. Do not explain the video. Rather draw out from your students their personal insights, feelings, reactions and questions regarding it.

We often find worksheets very useful to help youngsters respond to a video. For example, we ask them to draw the one image in the video that moved them most, that lingers in their memory. Or we ask them to write one thing they learned or want always to remember from the video.

Try using TV and videos. They have great catechetical potential. We hope our suggestions help.

31.

How Get Ready for Next Year?

"Classes are just ending for this year, but I already agreed to teach again next year. I'm really looking forward to the summer break, but I wonder if there aren't some things I could do to help me get ready for next year's teaching."

We admire your generosity and eagerness to prepare for next year.

Our first recommendation is to relax and enjoy the summer without being overly apprehensive about the next school year. Open yourself to the special opportunities the summer months may provide—a more relaxed pace, perhaps some travel to new places, closer contact with nature, fun time with family and friends. Summer can be a renewing, healing sacrament for our spirits.

While enjoying the summer, you might take a few relaxed steps to grow in knowledge of the *youngsters* and the *subject matter* you will teach. You might also expand your own personality by developing some new *skill* that may directly or indirectly help you be a more effective, creative catechist.

Knowledge of Young People

Here are several ways to grow in understanding of today's children and youth during the summer.

(1) Make the most of time with your and/or others' children and their friends. Children are normally around more during the summer since there is no school. Take advantage of your time with them. Listen to them. Talk with them. Do

things with them. Observe them when they are together. Notice what they like, how they interact, what interests them.

You can learn much about children and youth during the summer by enjoying your time with them in an observant, reflective way.

(2) Read children's books. Summer often provides opportunities for reading. This summer, read some good pieces of children's literature. Good books for children provide us adults with a precious window into the minds and hearts of young people of various ages. The better authors touch down into children's feelings, dreams, ideals, hurts, struggles, questions, abilities, challenges. Children's literature can be one of the most valuable, as well as delightful, ways of getting to know young people.

Turn to resources like Jim Trelease's *The New Read Aloud Handbook* (Penguin Books 1989), or Eden Ross Lipson's updated *The New York Times Parent's Guide to the Best Books for Children* (Times Books, 1991), or *The Horn Book Magazine* (14 Beacon Street, Boston, MA 02108). Ask at your local library or children's book store for these and other guides to fine children's books.

(3) Listen to the music young people love. Music is a privileged medium for understanding the young and their world. Music largely creates and defines the atmosphere in which today's young people live, the language they find understandable and meaningful. It provides adults with clues about what concerns, delights, frightens, comforts and challenges the children and youth we teach and love. It also can make you more aware of what messages they constantly receive.

Invite the youngsters in your life to guide you during the summer into the world of their music—some of which is genuinely beautiful and profound. Befriend someone who works in a record store as a source of leads on current hits. Use a resource like Don Kimball's *Top Music Countdown* (Cornerstone Media, P.O. Box 6236, Santa Rosa, CA 95406) to help you understand

and appreciate a world of music in which those you will teach feel very much at home. Some diocesan newspapers carry Charlie Martin's weekly feature on current popular music.

Knowledge of Subject Matter

Spend a half-hour or hour now as the school-year ends looking through the catechetical textbook you will be using next year. Notice the overriding theme—e.g., sacraments, morality, the Church—or some aspect of the content that really intrigues you or puzzles you—e.g., the parables of Jesus, Catholic social teaching, the Beatitudes.

Then find one or two good books, audio or videocassettes, on that subject. Read for your own understanding and appreciation—to update your awareness of developments in that area of theology and to fill your mind, heart and imagination with fresh insights, images and motivation. Ask your DRE and other catechists for suggestions. *Credence Cassettes* (115 E. Armour Blvd., Kansas City, MO. 64111) has video and audiocassettes on a wide variety of topics.

Develop Yourself and Your Skills

Summer can be a rare opportunity to take some time for yourself. It may be just a few minutes a day, an hour or two each week, or a weekend. Use the time for your own personal growth.

Some catechists focus on spiritual growth—reading the Bible, praying, keeping a journal, reading a professional book. Others learn something new and/or develop a skill that they have been wanting to learn—anything at all, maybe dancing, painting, sewing, cooking, playing the piano, using a computer.

These are just a few hints that might prove helpful in preparing for next year's teaching while enjoying the summer.

32.

Catechists' New Year's Resolutions?

"I'm sitting here preparing my first class of the year. Into my head out of nowhere pops the question, 'What resolutions are you going to make to be a better religion teacher this new year?' I started jotting notes, but decided to write you two instead. Any suggestions?"

What a great idea! New Year's resolutions for catechists! Here are a few we will make this year. Bounce them off your own experience.

(1) Decide to change the environment once a month or seasonally. Change the seating arrangement, the visuals, the routine of your lessons. Environmental change can add freshness and stimulation to your classes. Select visuals to create curiosity, invite questions, provide insights into key lesson themes, or related to liturgical seasons and feasts, and to current events.

(2) Read something regularly that will add to your professional growth. Read at least one good, up-to-date book on a theological topic related to what you are teaching, perhaps a book on Jesus, the Bible, sacraments, or Catholic social teachings.

One of the following magazines or newsletters read monthly will provide new insights and practical tips that can broaden your catechetical knowledge and skills—*Religion Teachers' Journal, Catechist, Catholic School Teacher, The Catechist's Connection, Momentum, The Living Light.* A variety of other monthly resources on Scripture, liturgy, and Church issues are readily available, as well as magazines targeted to specialized groups, like youth. Find one you like and read it faithfully each month.

(3) Get to know your students' families. It takes effort, but can be immensely rewarding, to become more closely acquainted with families of your students. Try preparing brief notes or letters for parents in which you share what you are teaching in each class, together with an idea or two for follow-up at home. Call each parent at least once during the class year. Have a parent-teacher meeting soon in the new year, and a family Mass for students and families a bit later.

(4) Meet together with one or more catechists monthly to share ideas and to plan ahead. Class-by-class planning for the coming month can make a big difference in your teaching. Planning with other catechists can be enriching and affirming. You will discover that each of you has creative ideas, individual strengths and weaknesses. Interaction sparks more good ideas than any one of you might generate alone. Planning a month ahead alerts you to things you may want to do or get beforehand.

(5) Invite a senior or other citizen in to dialogue with your students. We have found that few experiences have the power of bringing faith into relationship with life as does a guest who has experience in some area of life related to a lesson—e.g., a monk or nun sharing about monastic and religious life, an engaged or married couple, a Peace Corps volunteer, business person, artist or musician, laborer, or someone in charge of a shelter or soup kitchen. Be sure to let the youngsters ask questions and dialogue with the guest.

(6) Go to at least one catechetically-oriented meeting, lecture, workshop or congress. Many catechists find that such a gathering provides encouragement, support, and new ideas. There are so many opportunities—by audio- or videocassette if you find it impossible to be present physically.

(7) Consider a way to develop a personal word portrait of each student. Take a photo of each student. Place each picture on a blank sheet of paper. Then occasionally take some quiet time to reflect on each student. Note down what you know and like about each, what problems some may have, what talents each has, what you feel each needs most and can offer most to others. This can help you personalize your teaching.

(8) Commit yourself to writing a personal letter to each student at least once this year. Share in the letter why you like teaching her or him, what personal strengths and gifts you have noticed, something you've learned from him or her during the year. Do this on each student's birthday or name day, or on Valentine's Day, or other holiday. Such letters can create a special bond between you and each of your students.

(9) Determine to set aside one hour a week for lesson planning. Schedule it on your calendar. Besides planning a month ahead, preferably with one or more catechists, it is vital that you set aside an hour a week for final planning of the coming week's lesson. Try to do this as soon after the previous class as possible.

(10) Promise yourself that you will pray for each child before each class. Take a few moments before each class, perhaps as part of your weekly planning hour to call into your imagination each student's face as you pray briefly but personally for each one, that Christ may touch each through your teaching. Ask the Holy Spirit to help you genuinely to love each youngster you teach.

There are surely other New Year's resolutions for catechists. We hope our list stimulates you to make your own.

Bibliography

This brief bibliography highlights *practical* resources for catechists. It does not pretend to be complete, as the books to which it refers give ample listings of many other useful books, as well as media.

Official Church Documents

Vatican Council II: The Conciliar and Postconciliar Documents, ed. Austin Flannery (Costello Publishing, 1987)

National Conference of Catholic Bishops, *Sharing the Light of Faith—National Catechetical Directory for Catholics of the United States* (United States Catholic Conference, 1979)

Pope John Paul II, *Apostolic Exhortation on Catechesis* (United States Catholic Conference, 1979)

Vatican, *Catechism of the Catholic Church*, 1992.

Helpful Catechetical Books

Greg Dues, *Teaching Religion with Confidence and Joy* (Twenty-Third Publications, 1988)

Thomas H. Groome, *Christian Religious Education—Sharing Our Story and Vision* (Harper & Row, 1980); Thomas H. Groome, *Sharing Faith—A Comprehensive Approach to Religious Education & Pastoral Ministry* (Harper Collins, 1991)

Brennan R. Hill, *Key Dimensions of Religious Education* (St. Mary's Press, 1988)

Janaan Manternach and Carl J. Pfeifer, *Creative Catechist,* revised, expanded edition (Twenty-Third Publications, 1991)

Janaan Manternach with Carl J. Pfeifer, *And the Children Pray* (Ave Maria Press, 1989)

Carl J. Pfeifer and Janaan Manternach, *How to be a Better Catechist* (Sheed & Ward, 1989)

Matias Preiswerk, *Educating in the Living Word* (Orbis Books, 1987)

Kevin Treston, *A New Vision of Religious Education* (Twenty-Third Publications, 1993)

Thomas P. Walters, *Making a Difference* (Sheed & Ward, 1986)

Periodicals

Catechist (2451 East River Road, Dayton, OH 45439)

The Catechists' Connection (PO Box 414293, Kansas City, MO 64141

Group's JR. HIGH MINISTRY (Box 407, Mt. Morris, IL 61054)

The Living Light (c/o Department of Education, USCC, 1312 Massachusetts Ave., NW, Washington, DC 20005)

Religion Teacher's Journal (PO Box 180, Mystic, CT 06355)

Today's Catholic Teacher (2451 East River Road, Dayton, OH 45439)